WHAT'S NORMAL ANYWAY?

The Keys to Unlocking Your Mental Well-Being

Yelena Fishman
BA, PGDipPsych, MPsych(Couns)

First published by Ultimate World Publishing 2022
Copyright © 2022 Yelena Fishman

ISBN

Paperback: 978-1-922714-81-7
Ebook: 978-1-922714-82-4

Yelena Fishman has asserted her rights under the Copyright, Designs and Patents Act 1988 to be identified as the author of this work. The information in this book is based on the author's experiences and opinions. The publisher specifically disclaims responsibility for any adverse consequences which may result from use of the information contained herein. Permission to use information has been sought by the author. Any breaches will be rectified in further editions of the book.

All rights reserved. No part of this publication may be reproduced, stored in or introduced into a retrieval system, or transmitted in any form, or by any means (electronic, mechanical, photocopying, recording or otherwise) without the prior written permission of the author. Any person who does any unauthorised act in relation to this publication may be liable to criminal prosecution and civil claims for damages. Enquiries should be made through the publisher.

Cover design: Ultimate World Publishing
Layout and typesetting: Ultimate World Publishing
Editor: Isabelle Russell
Cover photo license: Ribah-Shutterstock.com

Ultimate World Publishing
Diamond Creek,
Victoria Australia 3089
www.writeabook.com.au

Testimonials

Once I started reading this book, I could not stop. Yelena writes so beautifully, so passionately, and every word comes from such a non-judgmental and dedicated individual who has overcome many obstacles in life and is now passing down her wisdom and education from her own journey and professional career.

This book is bright, knowledgeable and inspiring. Every person would benefit from this read to gain an understanding of what mental health really is and that what they are feeling is okay.

From depression and anxiety to personality disorders, one in four of us experience mental health issues every year, especially in these strange and unsettling times, as more of us than ever are struggling to cope. This lively, accessible guide is comforting, reassuring and should be on everyone's reading list.

Sabina Broder
Parents Pathway Counsellor

What's Normal Anyway

As a mother of a teenager and a teacher throughout the six lockdowns in Melbourne due to the Covid-19 pandemic, I was very interested in empowering others with the knowledge of 'what they were feeling is normal' and where they can get help if they felt they needed it. Yelena's book does just this. It provides powerful insights into what can be considered normal and not so normal, while going into detail about how, why and when to get help. It goes a step further by explaining what to look for and what to expect when getting help. By providing a tool that helps others to help themselves especially after so many around the world have struggled through the events of the last few years truly shows how committed Yelena is to helping others.

Vania Tantirimudalige Don
Generalist Teacher

Yelena leads you gently with her own inspiring story and creates a bridge for you to overcome any fears or doubts about seeking help for your mental health. She then guides you through all aspects of what to look for in a therapist, the types of therapy, expectations of your progress, communication skills, getting help for a loved one – and becoming your own psychologist.

As I read this book, I felt like I was taken to a vast library of knowledge which both inspired and empowered me. It is clearly written, easy to comprehend and held my interest all the way through. This is a must-read for anyone seeking help for their mental wellbeing, and especially for people who are frightened to take that first step - it is a much-needed resource in today's world.

Heather Binns
Author, *There Is Nothing To Fear*

Testimonials

Yelena's personal journey and professional lens are invaluable in helping us access mental health pathways and promoting wellbeing. An accessible and valuable resource for navigating the mental health maze, this is an empowering and useful text which clarifies both psychological diagnosis and treatment frameworks in easy-to-understand terms and approaches to seeking help.

Yelena has managed to capture the confusions and frustrations of dealing with mental health concerns and offering a pathway towards empowerment. Her personal story and professional experience will help the reader take the stigma sting out of mental health concerns.

Peter Langdon
Clinical and Counselling Psychologist

Yelena has certainly succeeded in creating a book that distinguishes itself by crafting a comprehensive, clear and easy to read manual on when, why and how to seek professional help. An incredibly insightful book that is based on personal experience, current research and work with patients that provides a roadmap of steps, tools and practical information on how to proactively navigate the nuances of mental health in today's society. An engaging, relatable and motivating book that is a must read for anyone interested in the importance of wellbeing. This will be a terrific resource for those in the therapy communities, but especially for those outside of them. A book that I will most definitely be recommending to my colleagues, friends and family!

Anna Tesoriero
Generalist Teacher

Disclaimer

This publication is intended as a source of information only. It is not a substitute for direct psychological, psychiatric or medical advice, diagnosis or treatment. If such assistance is required, the services of a qualified and competent professional should be sought.

This book includes some elements of real clients' stories. However, the clients' identifying details, such as their age, gender or other significant details, were changed to protect their identity.

Although the author and publisher made every effort to ensure that the information in this book was correct at the time of publication, neither shall assume any responsibility for any errors, inaccuracies, omissions or inconsistencies herein.

No warranties, either expressed or implied, are made on the information provided. By reading this, you have agreed to the disclaimer.

Dedication

This book is dedicated to health professionals in general and mental health professionals in particular. I deeply acknowledge and appreciate the hard work that you put in every day and your commitment to your colleagues, your clients and to lifelong learning in the field of mental health. I am honoured to walk among you, knowing that we are making a difference every single day.

I also wish to dedicate this book to my GP of nearly a decade, Dr Peter J Stiebel, who passed away during the preparation of this book. Dr Stiebel was an attentive, humorous and caring doctor and he is greatly missed.

Contents

Dedication	ix
Introduction	1
PART 1	**7**
Chapter 1: The Power of Your Story	9
Chapter 2: The Power of Resilience	23
PART 2	**47**
Chapter 3: The Power of Knowledge	49
Chapter 4: The Power of Decision-Making	65
Chapter 5: The Power of Discernment	75
Chapter 6: The Power of Diversity	93
Chapter 7: The Power of Your Intuition	109
Chapter 8: The Power of Backing Yourself	123
Chapter 9: The Power of Courageous Communication	137
Chapter 10: The Power of Intentionality	159
Chapter 11: The Power of Stepping Back	169
Chapter 12: The Power of Self-Mastery	181
Afterword	191
About the Author	193
Acknowledgements	195
Speaker Bio	197

Introduction

This book was born in the midst of the Covid-19 pandemic in September 2021.

The city that has been my home for the last 20 years, Melbourne, Australia, was plunged into its sixth lockdown in 18 months and, understandably, people really struggled. Businesses closed, students were studying remotely, there was a curfew in place and many of us felt emotionally and mentally exhausted. Melbourne's six lockdowns totalled 262 days – the longest lockdown in the world.

We were all collectively trying to make sense of something that none of us had experienced before. I was suddenly in the exact same boat as my clients. I was feeling the uncertainty at the same time that they were feeling it and I juggled similar work-life commitments as them. It added an additional angle to my interactions with my clients – we laughed more at ourselves and at the situation as we tried to quickly learn the new technology of conducting sessions over video, and there was more compassion and understanding if plans had to be frequently changed at the last minute due to changing rules and regulations.

What's Normal Anyway

These were two intense years that showed that at the end of the day, we are all human.

During the lockdowns, I noticed how important it was for my clients to hear that what they were feeling and doing was normal and made a lot of sense in the context of the lockdowns. Things that, prior to the pandemic, might have been concerning all of a sudden made sense in the context of the pandemic where – all the events were cancelled, people were ordered not to leave their houses, people could not physically see friends or loved ones, there were shortages of essential items in the supermarkets and there was a daily reporting on the news of the number of infected people and those who had died. Some of my clients, who were usually optimistic and had coped well with the previous five lockdowns, became hopeless during the sixth. In a highly *abnormal* situation, such as lockdowns, it made sense that my clients' behaviours and emotions changed and fluctuated.

The sixth lockdown was my catalyst for writing this book. There was a big demand for psychological services and long waiting lists. I wanted to create a book that would be available to as many people as possible. Writing this book also gave *me* a sense of normalcy. It gave my mind a very welcome break from what was on the news and helped me to focus on the topic that I am so passionate about: sharing my knowledge and understanding of psychology.

This book is for anyone who is concerned about themselves or a loved one and not quite sure if what they are noticing or experiencing is worth talking to a mental health professional about. At times we all can feel doubt as to whether what we are going through is 'normal' or whether it requires an input of a professional. This is true not only in mental health, but also in physical health, sexual health, dental health and so on: *'Do I need to speak to someone about this, or will it improve on its own?'* is a question that we might ask ourselves on various topics.

Introduction

As there is a lot of stigma, misconceptions, myths and confusion when it comes to the field of mental health, I hope that this book will clear up the most common misconceptions and make it clearer for people to recognise:

- If they would benefit from an input of a mental health professional
- What mental health professional is the right one for them
- Where to find that mental health professional and
- How to make the most out of therapy for long-lasting results

The first part of this book contains some of my personal story. Psychologists rarely reveal aspects of their personal lives, but I hope that in sharing my story, it will help you to feel less alone in your struggles and that it will empower you to take those courageous first steps in seeking psychological support when you need it the most.

The second part describes in great detail a step-by-step process for getting the right assistance. You will find that most chapters challenge you to either consider things from a different perspective, or to do exercises that will extend you in different areas of your life, be it assertive communication or trusting your intuition and doing what is right for you – even if others disagree. Some people like to have plenty of space to jot down their thoughts and reflections instead of writing them in the book. If you are one of those people, feel free to download **the complimentary 'Ultimate Companion to *'What's Normal Anyway?'* from my website: www.yelena-fishman.com.au.** It lists all the reflection exercises with extra space to write your thoughts.

If anything in this book causes you distress or discomfort, please reach out to:

What's Normal Anyway

- A trusted adult
- A counsellor or physician
- A telephone and online support service in your area. In Australia, Lifeline is available 24/7 on 13 11 14. If you are outside of Australia, please look up a phone line that offers counselling and support in your country.

Also note that the recommendations in this book are focused on face-to-face meetings with professionals, but with telephone and video appointments becoming more common, please know that the same recommendations still apply.

Before we begin, as a true psychologist, I will get you to self-assess your awareness and knowledge of the topics that I cover in the book. This is for a bit of fun and you can compare your scores with the same assessment at the end of the book. Please rate from 0-10, with 0 = no knowledge and 10 = a whole lot of knowledge.

Introduction

Current level of awareness/knowledge: Before starting the book

Topic	Level of knowledge from 0-10
What is considered 'normal'?	
Signs that indicate that an assistance from a mental health professional is required	
Where to start in order to get professional help	
What other help is out there in addition to seeing a professional one-on-one	
Difference between psychologists, psychiatrists, counsellors, psychotherapists and life coaches	
Different types of psychological therapies that are currently available	
How to identify whether the mental health professional you are seeing is right for you	
Effective communication at home, at work or with friends and loved ones	
How to track your progress in therapy	
How and where to get help for a loved one	
How to become your own psychologist	
Helpful books, websites and articles that can further expand your knowledge	
Add up your scores for your total:	

PART 1

Chapter 1

The Power of Your Story

'Persistence and resilience only come from having been given the chance to work through difficult problems.'
— **Gever Tulley**

I decided to include a chapter on my personal story for a number of reasons:

- I have been lucky to grow up and live in three very different countries on three different continents. This has given me in-depth insight into the ways in which different societies operate and how the concept of what is 'normal' changes depending on social, cultural, religious, political and other factors. I am hopeful that in describing my experiences, I will be able to give you, the reader, a broader perspective of what is considered 'normal'. As you read my descriptions, I welcome you to start reflecting on how the stories and the concepts that I describe fit in with your life experiences and your understanding of what is 'normal'.

- People at times have a misconception that if someone is a psychologist, then they have already achieved their own personal development, they lead a 'perfected life' and now they are in a position where they can advise others. As you go through this chapter and the rest of the book, you will see that psychologists are human, just like you. We have fears and doubts, insecurities and stressful moments. Even with all of our training and degrees, we at times say the wrong thing or get cranky with our loved ones, and we are definitely still learning.
- I have added this section to give hope to others that no matter how bleak things seem at times, **things *can* turn around and they *can* improve. In fact, I believe that it is thanks to our challenges that we discover how resourceful, strong and determined we really are.**

Please be aware that the experiences that I describe of the different countries are my own experiences and the experiences of relevant family members as they recall them. These experiences are not necessarily shared by other people who currently live or lived in these countries. I am also mindful that situations in countries change as time goes by. What happened 30-50 years ago does not necessarily reflect the reality in a particular country today.

My communist and socialist roots

The first thing that anyone asks me when they meet me for the first time is: '*What is that accent?*' followed by, '*Where are you originally from?*' My answer is usually quick: '*I'm from Russia, and yes, the accent is a bit mixed.*'

The Power of Your Story

This is the short, quick, inaccurate answer. The real answer spans a few pages and you will now get a front seat in hearing it.

My story begins in the early 80s. I was born in the year 1982 in Kishinev, the capital city of Moldova in Eastern Europe. In case you're unfamiliar with the area, Moldova is located between Romania and Ukraine. It is *not* Russia, but when I was born it was part of the Union of Soviet Socialist Republics (USSR).

The former USSR – a communist, collectivist culture, where everything belonged to the government and people had nothing of their own (no private houses, no private businesses, no private factories or shops). This was a culture where one was expected to conform and not stand out. My 86-year-old grandmother to this day says that her goal in the USSR was *'to be like everyone else – not worse and not better.'* The idea was for everyone to be equal.

From the stories that my father told me, there was only one variety of shoe in the store. If you wanted a different type of shoe- it was tough luck! There were only basics in the grocery stores – milk, bread, basic types of meat. Foods such as lemons or olives were considered 'luxuries'. If you were in a high-level job or had connections, you could get those luxuries. Our family was lucky in that my mum was a bookkeeper at a food factory (an incredible job to have in the USSR), so from time to time she was able to get chocolates or other 'luxurious' foods.

Due to a housing shortage in the USSR, it was very normal for multiple generations to live together in the same apartment. We were seven people living in a two-bedroom apartment: my parents, my maternal grandparents, my younger sister, Olga, my mum's younger sister, Svetlana, and myself. These kinds of living arrangements were very typical for the USSR and, in many ways, they worked well, as family members assisted one another. For example, my mum's younger sister was 12 when I was born, and she was often left to look after me. I have a lot of fun childhood memories with my Aunt Sveta – sharing candy together or her picking me up from school. My grandfather left his job when I started school so he could look after me as well.

Family Portrait, from left to right: baby sister Olga, Mum Anna, Aunt Svetlana, Dad Yakov. Sitting: Grandma Bassia, Yelena at the age of four, and Grandpa Arsen.

I viewed the Soviet culture as having a very clear hierarchy. There was always someone 'at the top' that the others were scared of, like a manager at work or a teacher at school. From my perspective, children were at the bottom of the hierarchy. Children were expected to entertain themselves, respect authority and not talk back. There were quite a lot of rules about how children should behave and what is 'proper' and 'improper' behaviour. At school, especially, the rules were very strict. We always had to sit at the tables with a straight back, and arms folded one on top of another. If we wanted to answer a question, we were to lift one arm at a 90-degree angle and when the teacher called our name, we were to stand up and only then were we permitted to answer the question. If any adult entered the classroom while the class was in session, the entire class had to stand up and be seated only once the adult said that we could sit down. The expectations for academic excellence were high and by the second grade, I remember learning Pushkin's poems by heart and reciting the multiplication times tables.

School photo (1990) of Yelena in second grade in the USSR

Thankfully, I was good academically, so I was able to meet the school's expectations, and kept my head low. Growing up in the socialist USSR culture firmly planted in me characteristics such as being humble and hard-working. The Soviet cartoons that I grew up on emphasised character strengths such as being courteous and positive, being loyal to friends and not leaving friends in trouble. These were great values to grow up on.

Unfortunately, however, there was a discrepancy between what the Soviet Union stood for, what the movies and the cartoons portrayed and what was happening in reality. Although the socialist/communist system was supposedly implemented to remove social inequalities, there was a lot of both overt and covert persecution, stigmatisation and discrimination on a political level, cultural level and religious level. I come from a Jewish family, however for a very long time I did not even know that I was Jewish. In the former USSR, atheism was the preferred policy of the state and there was religious repression. According to a research article by Soskovets, Krasilnikov and Myrmina (2016): *'As a result of a deliberate policy of the authorities, religion was forced out of the public sphere and people's consciousness; churches were destroyed, the clergy lost their jobs, religious believers were turned into outcasts and were deprived of their right to believe in their God. People, openly speaking about their faith and belief in God, were often misunderstood and rejected by the atheist society.'* (p.4)

In addition to religious persecution and discrimination, there was discrimination against ethnic minorities. The Jewish people were one of the most hated and persecuted minorities in the USSR. The saying, translated into English, *'If there is no water you could use, the fault is with the dirty Jews,'* is definitely something that I heard growing up.

The Soviet Union made sure that people of different ethnicities were known and clearly identified. Surnames were the most obvious way to know the person's ethnicity, while their looks would at times be a hint. As if that were not enough, your ethnicity was also very clearly listed on your ID under 'nationality'.

In our case, under 'nationality' it stated 'Jewish', even though Judaism is not a nationality. Had it stated 'Moldovan' or even 'a USSR citizen', that would have been more accurate, but interestingly, Jewish people were a separate category. According to my dad, at school the nationalities of all the students in the classroom were listed in a large journal, where the teacher marked attendances and gave grades and at times the teacher would even ask each student to stand up and state their nationality. My dad then heard: 'Ukrainian, Moldovan, Russian, Belarusian' and perhaps one or two 'Jewish'. According to my dad, even his library card stated that he was Jewish. He grew up in the 1950s, 1960s and 1970s, well after the Second World War.

According to the literature review by Vinogradov (2010), *'Anti-Semitism and inescapable, meticulously documented nationality combined to make life difficult for Soviet Jews after WWII. For instance, various 'affirmative action' programs were established that legitimized discrimination against Jews while favouring other ethnic minorities' (p.63)*. My family members experienced the discrimination firsthand, including having their job applications rejected based on them being Jewish. Yet, amazingly, they picked themselves up, dusted themselves off and made the best of what they had.

I included this section to highlight some of the things that were considered perfectly 'normal' in the former USSR. Now, as an adult who has experienced life in other countries, I look back at and feel horrified that this conduct was deemed acceptable at the time.

Resilience in the face of challenges

Despite the racist, discriminatory and suppressing culture of the USSR, I had a great childhood thanks to my resilient and tight-knit family. My parents and grandparents sheltered myself and my younger sister from as much of the politics and the harshness that they could. I was also blessed to have a very large and loving extended family. I have only positive memories of family catchups: everyone gathering together, my uncles throwing me up in the air, my cousins playing games with me and summer stays at my paternal grandparents.

Summer holidays at grandparents' house, from left to right: Grandpa Simion (Shimon), Aunt Klarissa, Grandma Sonia (Sarah), Uncle Zinovii, Cousin Polina. In the front: Cousin Anna with Yelena at the age of seven.

I did not realise at the time how significant these positive early experiences were in providing me with a buffer for the challenges that were to come. Indeed, studies show that positive childhood experiences are a buffer against the effects of exposure to adverse childhood life experiences (e.g., Bethell, et.al., 2019). More information on this topic, including tips for nurturing positive childhood experiences, are available through Child and Adolescent Behavioural Health (www.childandadolescent.org/positive-childhood-experiences/).

A weird culture, a weird kid or weird parents?

With all the conflicting messages within the USSR, anything outside their 'norm' was considered weird. It was easy to get confused.

I remember asking my parents if I could do things that a part of me thought were really 'weird', like sleeping in cold weather on the concrete floor of our balcony. I wanted to sleep out in the fresh air under the stars and to my surprise, my parents had no issue with that! They put thick blankets on the floor, dressed me in warm clothes and I was overjoyed at being wrapped like a cocoon and sleeping out in the cold. It is only when I was older that I understood why my request did not sound odd to my parents. My mum told me that from the time that myself and my sister were babies, she regularly left us to sleep in our prams on the balcony, alone – even during the cold winter months. We lived on the third storey of a building. The lift did not always work, so my mum could not physically carry a baby and a heavy pram down three flights of stairs. Yet she wanted her kids to sleep in fresh air. It was absolutely normal, and even considered healthy, for us to sleep rugged up outside. Those who grew up in Eastern Europe or in Scandinavian countries are probably familiar with this practice.

But maybe my parents were still weird and did not quite fit the USSR 'norm'? At the age of seven I thought that there was definitely something very weird about my dad. Sometimes, I would walk past one of the bedrooms and see Dad sitting in complete darkness, with his head bowed down and eyes closed. I didn't understand what was going on and thought that this was bizarre. Everyone else was in the living room, enjoying a movie or some other TV program, while he was sitting by himself in a dark room in such an odd seating position. I also couldn't understand why no-one else was worried about him. They just let him sit alone in the dark when the rest of us were together in the living room. Didn't they think that something was wrong? Eventually, I worked up the courage and whispered into the darkened room: *'Dad, what are you doing?'* He lifted up his head and quietly said, *'Meditating'* and lowered his head again. I had absolutely no idea what he was talking about. Still confused, I walked away, and concluded that Dad was just 'weird'.

What about the Russian culture itself? How 'normal' is it?

Below are a few things that were, and still are, considered to be completely normal in the Soviet/Russian culture:

- During festivities, people eat Holodetz, a popular traditional Russian dish. It is a cold jelly dish with pieces of meat and vegetables.
- One is not allowed to whistle in the house due to a widely held superstitious belief that it will result in having no money.
- When someone is talking and the person listening sneezes in the middle of the sentence, this means that the speaker is telling the truth. The speaker literally excitedly announces, *'Na pravdu!'* (*'To truth!'*) when the sneeze occurs, like a Soviet lie detector.
- If you gift someone flowers, you must give an **odd number** of flowers. For example, if you bought 10 roses, you must separate them into odd-numbered bunches and place them into separate vases, for example three roses in one vase and seven in another.
- Before leaving the house to go on a family holiday, the entire household sits down in silence for a minute. You've got all your

bags packed, you're ready to leave the house for your vacation and then (usually, but not always) the head of the household says: *'Let's sit down for a moment before we hit the road'*. Even if you're eager to leave, everybody sits down, stare at one another for about a minute in silence, then get up and get out of the door. To people from a Soviet/Russian background this is considered perfectly normal. It is considered that the trip will be more successful if you do this and it gives family members a quiet moment to ensure that they did not forget anything before setting off.

MY LEARNINGS:

- In hindsight, my family's cohesion, resilience and my positive experiences in their company gave me confidence and a strong sense of belonging that acted as a buffer against future adverse events.

- Growing up in the Soviet culture taught me to be hard-working, and to strive for excellence. It instilled in me great values such as the importance of friendship but also the desire to be like everyone else and a strong inclination to not stand out.

- There are situations in life that are beyond our control. We must do the best we can with what we have.

REFLECTION POINTS

This book is titled *What's Normal Anyway?* to help you expand your understanding of concepts such as 'normal', 'abnormal', 'weird' or 'odd'. Based on my life story in the former USSR reflect below on the following points:

1. What appeared to you as odd and unusual in the story?

_____
_____
_____
_____
_____
_____
_____
_____

2. What segments seemed reasonable, familiar and 'normal' to you, if anything?

_____
_____
_____
_____
_____
_____
_____
_____

The Power of Your Story

Chances are that if you have had a similar cultural upbringing to me, then a lot of what I described would sound familiar and perhaps 'normal'. Reflect on your own cultural upbringing and background and examine the lenses through which you are deciding what is considered 'normal' or 'abnormal'. There is no judgement here. Rather, it is about expanding your own understanding and perception.

References:

Bethell, C., Jones, J., Gombojav,N., Linkenbach, J., Sege, R. (2019). Positive childhood experiences and adult mental and relational health in a statewide sample: Associations across adverse childhood experiences levels. *Jama Pediatrics, 173*(11). https://doi:10.1001/jamapediatrics.2019.3007.

Kreitz, M. *Positive Childhood Experiences.* Child and Adolescent Behavioural Health. www.childandadolescent.org/positive-childhood-experiences/

Soskovets, L., Krasilnikov, S., & Myrmina, D. (2016). Persecution of believers as a systemic feature of the Soviet regime. *SHS Web of Conferences, 28*, 1-4. https://doi: 10.1051/shsconf/20162801098

Vinogradov A. (2010). Religion and nationality: The transformation of Jewish identity in the Soviet Union. *Penn History Review, 18* (1), Article 5, 50-69.

Chapter 2

The Power of Resilience

'If you are lucky enough to never experience any sort of adversity, we won't know how resilient you are. It's only when you're faced with obstacles, stress, and other environmental threats that resilience, or the lack of it, emerges: Do you succumb or do you surmount?'

— **Maria Konnikova**

In the previous chapter, I discussed how the experiences and the challenges in our lives can actually be blessings in disguise, as they show us how resourceful and capable we truly are. I focused on the challenges of the adults in my family, who were facing constant discrimination in a country where they were born, yet they were blatantly singled out as 'foreign'.

What's Normal Anyway

For the majority of the USSR's existence, its borders were closed so most people could not leave and had to manage the best they could under the Soviet regime. However, from about 1989, the collapse of USSR began. I was seven years old at the time and wasn't exposed to any political information, but by 1990-1991 there were definite changes that were happening – all of a sudden, the American cartoon *Chip 'n' Dale* was showing on TV and we could get American chewing gum! I could also tell that there was more tension and anxiety in the house and the adults were worried and were preparing for something big to occur. The fact that I did not know what they were worried about got me to imagine worst case scenarios, like a possible war and food shortage. However, for the most part, I was still enjoying a carefree childhood of attending school and playing outside with my friends.

This chapter will take you through the biggest change that I experienced as a young child and possibly the biggest challenge that my family faced. In my opinion, none of us were really prepared for it. For me, this challenging life phase was a catalyst to my development, and it is the reason that I've chosen to become a psychologist. As you are reading through this chapter, I would encourage you to reflect on the most difficult moments that you have had in your life so far, and the fact that you are still here. If you are going through a tough time right now, I hope that this chapter will give you the motivation to keep going and not give up.

Migration to the Holy Land

In August 1990, my aunt Svetlana had her wedding in Kishinev. This was the very last time that I remember seeing my entire extended family together in the same place. The USSR officially dissolved in December 1991, but from the time of my aunt's wedding, some of our relatives already started to leave the country. The borders were

The Power of Resilience

opening up and people were escaping! Most of the first ones to leave were people of Jewish descent, and after what I have described to you, I think you can understand why. We already had family living in Melbourne, Australia since the 1970s and my grandfather hoped to move there. Another escape option that was open to us was to migrate to Israel. Being the only Jewish country in the world, Jewish migrants would get automatic citizenship and new arrivals received financial assistance to help them settle in.

Our tight-knit extended family was split in half. Half came to Australia as refugees, while the other half migrated to Israel. In the blink of an eye, myself, my sister and my parents lost the support of the extended family that we had all enjoyed in the USSR and in an instant, we ended up in a country where people spoke a language that we did not know and had cultural mannerisms that were foreign to us all.

As a nine-year-old child, I did not really understand the concept of migration, and did not know what Israel would be like. I imagined palm trees, bananas and dark-skinned women carrying woven baskets on their heads. I was also certain that all the Jews in Israel abided by the Ten Commandments and I was excited to see what that would be like. My dad's parents, his sister and her family migrated a year before us to the town of Kiriat Haim, near Haifa, and we settled there too, to be close to them. I felt happy to be reunited with them and was excited to try bananas in Israel as I had never seen any tropical fruits in Moldova.

What's Normal Anyway

Arrival to Israel, August 1991. Yelena with her mother, Anna, sister Olga, grandparents Sonia and Simion, and cousin Polina

However, my happiness was very short-lived. Israel is a small country that all of a sudden had to accommodate a migration of almost two million Jews from the USSR in the 1990s. It is a melting pot of many different cultures and, in my perception, our arrival was like a thorn for the locals. My parents, sister and I had no prior exposure to the local language, we did not know any of the Jewish customs (as back in the USSR religion was repressed) and the hot climate was so different to the pleasant, cool climate that we were used to. The way that we dressed, as well as our mannerisms, immediately distinguished us from the locals. I think that wearing socks with sandals was the quickest giveaway. Once again, we were the strange foreigners – not belonging to the country where we were born, nor to the country that we migrated to.

Did you know?

A lot of research was conducted on the topic of migration and mental health of the migrants. For example, the literature review by Virupaksha, Kumar and Nirmala (2014) acknowledged that: *'Migration…is a process. Many times, lack of preparedness, difficulties in adjusting to the new environment, the complexity of the local system, language difficulties, cultural disparities and adverse experiences would cause distress to the migrants…subsequently, it has a negative impact on mental well-being of such population.'* (p.233).

Of specific relevance to the rest of this chapter is an Israeli study (Shoshani, et al., 2016), that compared native-born Israeli teenagers and groups of teenagers who were born in Israel to migrant parents (one-and-a-half and second-generation migrant teenagers). The researchers compared the groups on measurements of school engagement, behavioural risk-taking and mental health. *'The research findings revealed substantially higher levels of mental health symptoms and risk behaviours among migrant groups compared with native-born adolescents'* (p.181). These results are consistent with previous studies, which indicated that *'migration may be a risk factor for psychological maladjustment and engagement in risk behaviors among youth from immigrant families'* (p.192). In this study, the migrant sample included teenagers from a variety of countries, not specifically the former USSR. However, keep in mind the findings of this study as you continue to read this chapter.

What's Normal Anyway

New reality

We arrived in Israel in the middle of August. Two weeks later came September 1st, the first day of school for children in the northern hemisphere. My sister was five years old and was sent to a local kindergarten where they changed her name from Olga to a local-sounding name, Orit. This was standard practice at the time, but being older, I was able to refuse an alteration to my name. When my sister started school, she went back to her original name.

I was nine years old and was sent to a local primary school. While some people were really lovely and welcoming when I started school, the overall reception of migrants from the former USSR was quite hostile. From the first day of school there was daily bullying and harassment from the boys. I was told to *'go back to Russia'*, called *'smelly Russian'* and was regularly threatened to get beaten up after school. The girls were kinder and made an effort to include me. Outside of school, the bullying and the harassment continued from complete strangers, both adults and children. I remember walking along a street and a random guy, aged perhaps 25, passed me by and remarked, *'Four-eyed!'* as I wore glasses at the time. I was about 11 or 12 years old.

On another occasion, a teenager, perhaps a year or two older than me, passed by me and called me *'fat'* for no reason whatsoever. I wasn't even overweight and by the time I got over the shock of such an unexpected remark, he was already far away. Unfortunately, these types of comments as well as sexual harassment in the form of constant wolf whistling or blatant sexualised statements, were a daily occurrence.

Sadly, children with the lighter features such as blonde hair and blue eyes were especially targeted with vicious attacks. The girls were called *'sluts/prostitutes'* and were subjected to inappropriate offers or comments. The boys were referred to as *'alcoholics'* and

The Power of Resilience

'Russian mafia'. The responsible adults were absent for most of this, including teachers or parents of the bullies. Our parents already had a lot on their plates, adjusting to a new country, finding work and learning a foreign language. The way I saw it, we, the bullied kids, were on our own.

Having dark hair and eyes was an advantage for me in that I received less bullying than my friends with lighter features. However, I still received a constant barrage of sexual harassment outside of school and constant bullying at school – just like the rest of us *'Russians'*.

With my parents being busy working and settling into the new country, from the age of nine I found myself in the role of 'the responsible adult', whose job it was to ensure that my sister and I got to and from school safely, completed homework, cleaned the house and got ourselves fed. We were home alone every day till 8.30 pm. Although this made me grow up much faster, it also helped my sister and I foster a really close relationship. We made up many games together, got up to a lot of childhood mischief and learned how to fight and then make up without adult intervention. We made our home a safe sanctuary from the hostile treatment that many former USSR migrants received 'out in the open'.

What's Normal Anyway

Yelena and Olga laughing together

However, I began to change. From a formerly popular girl with a mischievous sense of humour in the USSR, I became withdrawn and silent. Outside of school, it was pretty much just my sister and I. I consider myself very lucky that I have her.

The Power of Resilience

These traumas affected each of us differently. I cannot speak on behalf of everyone, but from my experience, as the years went by, a few of my young blonde female friends and our male friends became more ostracised, hung around only Russian-speaking migrants, smoked, drank alcohol and got into trouble.

Inventing my identity in the new, chaotic world

I definitely did not want to go down the destructive path of some of my friends, so I withdrew from them. I was good academically and living in the USSR gave me a 'head-start' training to be diligent, studious and to not stand out. So, I decided to channel all my focus into my studies and adopted an identity of 'the geek'. Being a geek fitted me perfectly. This way, I could blend into the new hostile background and be invisible, which felt like the safest option in a new world full of landmines. I did not say a word during classes, as any mispronunciations were met with roars of laughter from the classmates.

Gloomy days

As the years in Israel progressed, the adjustment did not get any easier. When I started high school, things got even gloomier. There was only one high school in the area where my family had settled, and it was large and old. The walls were peeling and there were iron bars on all the windows. It looked and felt like a prison. The boys in our year level became even more feral and uncontrollable than they were during primary school years. Our teacher and principal could not regain any control over them. Rather than making these issues a problem for the adults to resolve, those in authority expected the quiet female students to exert influence over these rowdy, uncontrollable boys. It was a disaster.

What's Normal Anyway

As Year 8 progressed into Year 9, the pressure at school became more noticeable. The teachers were preparing us for important exams in Year 10. I, of course wanted to do well, fully embodying my geek persona. I placed all my eggs into the academic basket and the pressure was getting to me. I remember bursting into tears in class after receiving back my math test. I scored 99 on it and couldn't believe that I had made a mistake somewhere to lose a single point. The bullies were, of course, right there, saying things like, *'Aww, is Daddy going to beat you up at home for getting 99 instead of 100?'* It all happened right in front of the teacher, yet she did not even approach us to ask what was going on or to ask me why I was crying.

We had two school counsellors and the room of one of them was right next to my class. For a minute I considered seeing her, but her door was always closed and there was no information on the door informing when she was available to see students. I also was not sure whether what I went through warranted seeing her. One of my friends was seeing a school counsellor at the time, but I thought to myself: *'My friend's mum is a single mum and they have financial issues. I can understand why it's good for my friend to speak to the counsellor, but I'm not sure if I really need to see one'.*

Now, as an adult and a psychologist, I can see how irresponsible it was of the teachers to not intervene when a student was being bullied in front of them, and to not even approach a distressed student to offer them comfort and assistance. Additionally, it also does not make sense to me, why even though the school counsellor's room was right next to my class, no one ever introduced her to the students or explained how students could see her or why someone might benefit from seeing her.

The Power of Resilience

Breaking point

I felt completely alone around this time and even my friends started noticing that something was not quite right, but they did not know how to approach it. I was more irritable and would get easily upset or angry over minor things. I also started getting frequent bouts of viruses and for the first time in many years saw a GP. He checked me over, asked me what the problem was, and I said that school was stressful. I did not say anything else. It was only later that I learned that there was a direct connection between my low state of mind, high stress levels and what was happening with my body. Biologically, stress is intended to be a short-term – an 'emergency' response – to a threat in the environment. During the stress response, some bodily systems are temporarily shut down or suppressed in order to conserve energy – such as the reproductive system, digestive system and immune system. This is why when we feel stressed for a long period of time, we are more susceptible to viruses and may also notice digestive, menstrual and sexual issues, along with headaches and neck or other muscle pain.

An interesting thing is that the brain does **not** differentiate between physical threat, emotional threat, social threat, financial threat or even real and imaginary threats. As far as the brain is concerned- every threat gets the exact same biological response. Whether you are chased by a tiger, watch a horror movie, have $1,000 stolen from your account, or subjected to social rejection – your brain will release the same stress hormones and the hormones will trigger the same physiological response in your body. How long will the response last? That depends on how long the real or perceived threat persists. Your brain will continue to release the stress hormones until it believes that you are **physically safe.**

In my case, I was dealing with daily stress for prolonged hours of the day. It was akin to me phoning emergency services multiple times a day to rescue me from events that I couldn't actually escape from. Both myself and my 'emergency' response were fatigued from this, and the frequent bouts of colds and viruses were my body's way of letting me know this.

A lot of research was conducted in the area of chronic stress. The American Psychological Association (2018) has a great summary of the range of health problems that chronic stress can lead to, as well as simple strategies to reduce stress levels, such as through physical exercise, muscle relaxation, regular intake of water and healthy food, breathing techniques and potentially seeing a therapist for additional cognitive and behavioural strategies: www.apa.org/topics/stress/body.

Attempts to get psychological help

As things continued to go downhill, one evening when both my parents were in the living room, I suddenly blurted out to Mum, *'I think I need to see a psychologist.'* She instantly replied, *'Don't be ridiculous.'* A few seconds later, she asked why I would need a psychologist, but by that stage I had composed myself and replied that I just want to understand myself more. In many traditional cultures, seeing a psychologist or a psychiatrist carries a strong stigma. My mum's response made sense in the context of her upbringing and the culture of the former USSR. She gave me a book by Dale Carnegie, titled *How to Win Friends and Influence People*, which was a book that she enjoyed. It was a nice read, but the strategies did not help me. I kept being verbally bullied at school by the other students. I ignored them all and kept putting pressure on myself to do *really* well in every single subject. The harassment and the bullying by complete strangers outside of school continued as well and I started to run out of coping mechanisms.

The Power of Resilience

It was around that time that thoughts about death and dying began to enter my mind. For an entire year, every night there was an internal conversation in my mind, where one side was practically begging for me to end my life and the more time passed, the more desperate and even angry that part grew. It would say things like, '*What are you waiting for? You know that tomorrow you'll wake up and it all will be the same.*' The other part of me was silently listening – feeling the pain of the hurting part and shedding tears with it – but not arguing back. The hurting part was right in that nothing changed from day-to-day, so its distress was understandable. Many years later, I learned that this was a common occurrence for people who contemplated suicide to experience this 'ambivalence' – where one part of the person wished to end their emotional pain by ending their life while another part resisted the negative dialogue. This ambivalence is well documented in research (e.g., Bryan, 2020) and is acknowledged by services that support individuals who are contemplating suicide or support families and friends who are bereaved by suicide. At the end of this chapter, I have listed the details of such support services.

> '*The greater the obstacle, the more glory in overcoming it.*'
> – **Moliere**

In hindsight, challenging experiences allowed me to delve even deeper into myself, and to discover resilience that carries me to this day. If you ever went through anything very challenging, I hope that when you look back on that difficult time, it also gives you renewed strength and confidence to know that you can overcome other tough times. And if you are going through a tough time right now, I hope that you will continue reading on and seek out the necessary support.

Blessings in challenging times

Although I felt alone and desperate, I was very fortunate to have my sister and another close friend. They did not know the extent of my distress, but despite noticing that I was more irritable and not quite myself, they were there and we shared jokes with each other, listened to popular music of the 1990s, and came up with fun things to do together. Their presence made a very positive difference. We all want to feel that we belong somewhere and that somebody cares. Having a social support network can be instrumental in getting through a bad time, even if the people in the network do not know exactly what to say or what to do to assist in a challenging situation. A great summary of the benefits of social support on psychological health was written by Kendra Cherry (2020) and available to be viewed at: www.verywellmind.com/social-support-for-psychological-health-4119970.

I also aimed to keep a predictable routine and engage in things that I enjoyed, such as attending piano lessons, which I absolutely loved. They gave me mental respite and a sense of achievement outside of my academic studies. I also took comfort in watching classic movies from the Soviet era, which included a lot of singing and dancing and were very uplifting. During Melbourne's covid-19 lockdowns, I used the exact same strategy to keep my spirits up. There's a lot of comfort in watching a familiar movie during an uncertain time, as you know for certain how your beloved movie will end.

The Power of Resilience

Yelena (centre), aged approximately 13, with her sister, Olga, and her mother at a local beach.

The book that saved my life

When the summer holidays between Year 9 and Year 10 started, I decided that a serious change was needed in relation to how I was feeling. I looked around the house for any books that would help. Thankfully, my dad was still very much into meditation and self-development. Around the time that I was going through my difficulties, he was attending many seminars and self-development workshops. He would come home in the evenings and tell us about the topics of discussion and I sat there with my eyes wide open, listening to everything that he learned.

Out of the many books that he brought back home I decided to start by reading *Happiness and Personal Problems: Psychology Made Easy* by Chuck T. Falcon, translated into Russian.

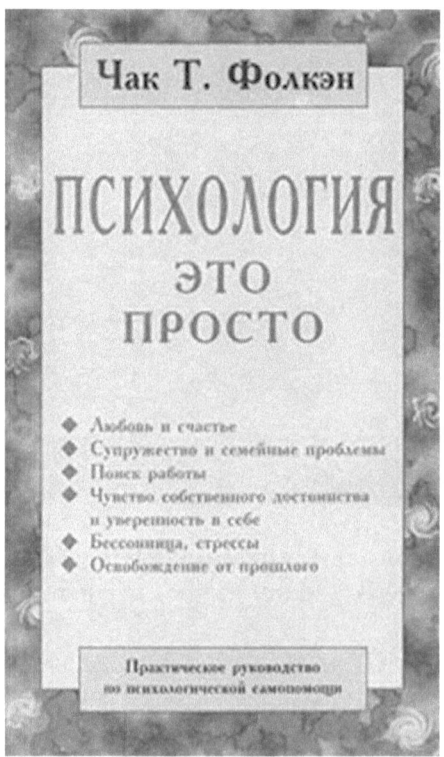

Book Cover by Chuck T. Falcon in Russian

I opened the book and looked over the glossary of chapters. There were many chapters that were not relevant to me; however, there was one chapter that immediately caught my attention and the one that I decided to read first. It was the chapter about suicidal thinking. I got more than what I had bargained for in this chapter.

When I opened the chapter, it was as if Chuck was inside of my head, reading my exact thoughts and responding to them. The first thing that I remember reading in this chapter was: *'If you are visualising your funeral and you have a plan how to* end *your life, then you are at a high risk of committing suicide.'* My jaw dropped and it was the first time that someone had ever told me how serious my thoughts were. Until that moment, I thought that my thoughts were just thoughts of a person feeling sad and going through sad things. I did not comprehend the full severity of the situation. This book was the adult that I needed in my life.

Although Chuck said that my symptoms matched the diagnosis of clinical depression, I was not in any hurry to diagnose myself. I'll paraphrase a quote by Debi Hope: *'Before you diagnose yourself with depression or low self-esteem, first make sure that you are not surrounded by idiots.'* Even at the age of 15, I absolutely knew that my symptoms were a direct result of being surrounded by idiots for seven years. No wonder I was at breaking point!

I will note here that from what I saw online, the Russian translation of the book is still available for purchase. Years later, I also bought the English version of the book.

Book cover by Chuck T. Falcon in English

When I recommended it to clients, they could not find this version of the book. Online there is a later version, with a blue cover from the year 1999.

Walking with Chuck

Over the next two months of the summer holidays, I stayed at home and spent every day reading the chapters of this book, taking in the information and the many interesting metaphors that the author included. Chuck wrote about the importance of becoming your own best friend and making the inner chatter (that we all have) supportive and encouraging rather than a barrage of relentless criticism. He compared each negative thought to one kilogram of weight and asked the reader to reflect on how heavy the load must feel the more we carry negative thoughts around with us.

At the time of the book being published, in 1992, Cognitive Behavioural Therapy (CBT), founded by Dr Aaron Beck, was the leading therapy for depression and automatic negative thinking patterns. Without mentioning the name of this type of therapy, Chuck walked me through CBT techniques, gently challenging my automatic negative thinking.

Chuck wrote his book so skilfully that it felt as if he was in front of me, directly answering every objection that I had in my mind. Below are paraphrases of the Russian translation that I had at home, as my 15-year-old self remembered them.

In one such section, Chuck wrote something along the lines of, *'You must be thinking that your anger, your resentment and negativity is because 'they' caused it, whomever 'they' are.'*

I eagerly nodded my head *'yes'* and Chuck continued, *'That's what a lot of people think, but in fact, no. 'They' could not have caused you to feel anything.'*

You should have seen my mortified face. What was he saying?

Chuck continued again: *'You'll probably say to me: 'You don't understand! You don't know how badly they treated me. If you knew what they had done and what they had said, you would understand that my anger, resentment and negative thinking is* because *of 'them'.'* I vigorously nodded again. *Yes, exactly!* I thought. *If it weren't for those bullies, I wouldn't be in the psychological state that I was in.*

What's Normal Anyway

Chuck then went on to explain: *'You think that how you feel is because what someone had said or done to you, but in fact, **no one** can make you feel a certain way. No one else lives in your head, no one else talks to you in your head. I am sure that what they have done to you was awful, insensitive and hurtful. They are responsible **for their words and actions**. However, the **feelings** that their words and actions evoked in you, are your responsibility. Why are you giving them control by allowing them to impact on your feelings?'* His words made me reflect.

The sections on self-image and comparing ourselves to others were also fascinating. I have included here two of his metaphors on the topic that I especially loved and that made me reflect on my situation. Firstly:

*'There will always be someone who is smarter than you, taller than you, more beautiful than you, more successful than you are. It is completely pointless to compare yourself to someone else. Imagine this scenario: You are a fast runner and you want to compete against a horse. Would you agree that the horse is faster than you? Would you agree that no matter how much and how hard you train, you will **never** outrun a horse? **Never**. Are you going to be upset about a horse running faster than you? No. This is ridiculous! It's a horse that you're comparing yourself to. Can you see how ridiculous it is to be upset over not being able to outrun a horse?'*

The second metaphor on this same topic was the following:

'Imagine that you can see in front of you two trees. One tree is tall and the other tree is short. Which tree is better, the tall one or the short one? How can you answer this question? It is a ridiculous question. They are just trees. Neither of them is better. One is tall and the other one is short.'

The point of these metaphors was to highlight how ridiculous humans are in comparing themselves to one another.

Finding my life's mission

As I kept reading this incredible book and applying Chuck's strategies to my own life, I found myself thinking: *'This information is so easy! I must share it with others!'*. That's when I decided that I would become a psychologist. I wanted to help others to demystify psychology and empower them with simple and easy strategies the way Chuck empowered me with his book.

> *'Legacy is not what I did for myself. It's what I'm doing for the next generation.'*
> **– Vitor Belfort**

MY LEARNINGS:

- The darkest moments of your life have the potential to uncover strengths that you did not know existed.

- Never give up as you don't know what is on the other side of your challenges.

- People who stay by your side even when you 'lose your sparkle' are to be treasured. They might not be able to change or fix anything, but their presence is significant.

Migration number two: moving to Australia and making my dream come true

After two months of Chuck walking alongside me, I felt like a new person. I was more confident, happier, reconnected with my old friends and made new friendships that have thrived to this day. However, my mum was less happy. Her parents and sister were in faraway Australia and she wanted to spend as much time with them as possible. So, after a decade of living in Israel, our family made a second migration to Australia.

After finally feeling settled in, a second migration, this time at the age of 19, was heartbreaking as I felt sad to leave my friends behind. However, this was also my chance to make my dream of becoming a psychologist a reality, by taking the next big step and enrolling into a university in Melbourne.

The move required additional adjustments, such as overcoming self-doubts about studying psychology in the English language, making new friends and starting life once again in a foreign country. However, this definitely was the best step, and out of all the countries where I lived, Australia feels like a real home. People still ask about my accent and correct my pronunciation, but it is always from a genuine wish to understand and help me improve, never from malice. I am truly blessed to live in a place where I can be myself – even with my odd accent, my pronunciation that is a mix of American and Australian English, Russian and Hebrew, and the mistakes that I make in every language even though I'm supposed to know them all fluently.

SUMMARY

In the last two chapters, I outlined behaviours that could be considered either within the norm or outside the norm, depending on the context and cultural nuances of the behaviour. It was important for me to also show how even suicidal thinking, which is a clear risk factor, can still be understandable when the full context of the situation is taken into account.

In the following chapters, we will delve deeper into recognising when it is appropriate for a person to see a mental health specialist. My hope is that *What's Normal Anyway?* will be the book that will take another person by the hand from a place of confusion to a place of clarity and empowerment, just as Chuck T. Falcon did for me.

Additional resources:

Below are resources for anyone who may need support around the topic of suicide. Although the services are based in Australia, the information can be accessed online. A Google search can reveal services in your local area that may also assist.

Suicide Call Back Service is a nationwide service providing 24/7 telephone and online counselling to people affected by suicide. https://www.suicidecallbackservice.org.au. Phone number: 1300 659 467

Lifeline Australia – a national charity providing all Australians experiencing a personal crisis with access to 24-hour crisis support and suicide prevention. Phone number: 13 11 14. https://www.lifeline.org.au

Suicide Bereavement Support – Support After Suicide

StandBy is accessible 24 hours a day, seven days a week. Free face-to-face or phone support; free suicide bereavement resources online; support packs; toolkits and children's books. Phone number: 1300 727 247; https://www.standbysupport.com.au/suicide/support

References:

American Psychological Association. (2018). *Stress effects on the body.* www.apa.org/topics/stress/body

Bryan, C. J. (2020). The temporal dynamics of the wish to live and the wish to die among suicidal individuals. In A.C. Page & W. G. K. Stritzke (Eds.), *Alternatives to suicide: Beyond risk and toward a life worth living* (pp.71-88). Elsevier Academic Press. https://doi.org/10.1016/B978-0-12-814297-4.00004-2

Cherry, Kendra. (2020). *How Social Support Contributes to Psychological Health.* www.verywellmind.com/social-support-for-psychological-health-4119970.

Falcon, C.T., (1992). *Happiness and Personal Problems: Psychology Made Easy.* Sensible Psychology Pr; 1st ed.

Shoshani, A., Nakash, O., Harper, R.A., & Zubiba, H. (2016). School engagement, acculturation, and mental health among migrant adolescents in Israel. *School Psychology Quarterly, 31*(2), 181- 197. https://dx.doi.org/10.1037/spq0000133

Virupaksha, H. G., Kumar, A., Nirmala, B.P. (2014). Migration and mental health: An interface. *Journal of Natural Science, Biology and Medicine, 5*(2), 233-239.

PART 2

Chapter 3

The Power of Knowledge

Recapping Part 1, you now know that what is considered 'normal' is not a straightforward answer. What is 'normal' depends on many factors, such as:

- The cultural and political climate that you live in
- Gender roles and expectations
- Societal attitudes towards different behaviours
- Life experiences
- Your personality and usual behavioural patterns

If you are usually a quiet, shy person who prefers to stay at home with a good book and a few close friends and then all of a sudden you are off to a wild party every night with complete strangers, that would be out of character for you. If this is combined with other things that are unusual for you, people around you might get worried that something is not quite right. Perhaps you're just going through a phase in your life when you want to try something different for yourself and perhaps there is a reason for concern. How will you know the difference?

This chapter will address the following question: *Is what I'm feeling a reason for concern? Do I actually need professional help?*

It will give you a general overview of the world of psychology and how mental health professionals make their decision on whether something falls outside the 'norm'. In clinical language, we refer to this as 'formulation' and 'intake triage questions'.

Your reasons for reading this chapter

There could be a number of reasons why you might be interested in understanding in more depth whether your or someone else's behaviour is a cause for concern:

1. You're a parent of a teenager or a young person – You know what life was like when you were growing up. Your parents and the society had particular expectations of you and the rules were familiar. However, things have changed so much in the last 20 years. The rapid expansion of technology and a range of social media platforms make this truly a new world. So, it can be tricky to ascertain what is 'normal' for this age group when your 'normal' looked very different. It is indeed a fine line to walk for any parent. On the one hand you might not want to make a big deal out of something that might not be an actual problem, but on the other hand you want to make sure that your child is not in trouble. How will you know? Based on the information in this chapter, you can at least have a starting point and an indication as to whether there really is a reason for concern.

The Power of Knowledge

A growing body of scientific research on the topic of brain neurology suggests that the critical parts of the brain that are responsible for decision-making do not fully mature until about the age of 25 for boys and around the age of 21-23 for girls (Aamondt & Wang, 2012; Arain et al., 2013). This is important for both parents and young people to keep in mind in order to adjust their expectations, extend compassion and perhaps even reduce some of the pressure on young people to act as adults, as biologically their brains will continue to develop until their early-mid 20s. This does not mean letting young people off the hook when they cross boundaries, but more about taking into account the volume of information and new pressures that they need to deal with while their brains are still developing.

2. You're a young person – Dealing with the pressures of academic studies, navigating relationships, friendships and adjusting to a range of biological and hormonal changes can be a lot. In fact, according to SANE Australia, a national mental health charity, *'More than 70 per cent of mental illnesses will emerge for the first time by* **the age of 25** *(bold in the original)'* (www.sane.org; Factsheets, 'Mental health issues in younger people').

Indeed, the period from puberty till about the age of 25 is a considerably turbulent period, where the young person is trying to 'find their place' in the world, striving to figure out their identity, decide on a career path and navigate often multiple sources of influence: parents, teachers, friends, social media influencers and so on.

However, just because you are a young person going through a challenging time does not automatically mean that you have a diagnosable mental illness. Once again, it all depends on the context and the extent of the behaviour. So, please, don't get ahead of yourself and start catastrophising or self-diagnosing. This book is intended to help you learn whether there is indeed a reason for professional intervention and where to get it.

3. You're an adult going through a period of high stress, or some type of an adjustment in your life – Perhaps you're an overworked parent of young children, balancing working hours with the wish to be present for your children. Alternatively, you could be reaching the point of retirement and wondering what the rest of your life is going to be like, or anything in between.

You've got a decision to make

We're barely through the start of this chapter and you might already be feeling some discomfort or anxiety about what you have read so far.

Potentially, you're wondering if you or your teenager are 'too precious' and just need to toughen up and get on with things! If we look historically, the message for most of us born in the last century indeed was: *'Just keep going.'* Things were difficult for everyone, there was no luxury to stop and consider feelings, to sit with a counsellor for an hour to talk about challenges. You kept going until things got too much and then you kept going some more.

In some places and cultures around the world this is still the case. I am certain that you have gotten through a lot in your life already, most likely without any assistance and without talking about things with a stranger.

And yet, we are living in a different world to the one that we grew up in. In this world, people are growing sick of shoving down their feelings, putting on a fake smile for others and pretending it didn't hurt. In this world, parents reflect on how they were raised and they

The Power of Knowledge

want to do better for their children. Even though it is foreign and uncomfortable, for the first time in 30, 40 or 50 years, people start to deepen their understanding of their emotions, improve the way that they speak to their partners and change the way that they respond to their children. Amazingly, it takes only one person in the family to decide that enough is enough and this decision can change the life trajectory not only for themselves but also for those around them.

As we go through this book, I will continue addressing uncertainties and anxieties that might come up with every step in the journey of seeking help. They are all absolutely normal. Implement what you can now, as every step in the right direction is already progress.

> *'The only courage that matters is the kind that takes you from one moment to the next.'*
> **– Mignon McLaughlin**

To orient you to the process of how professionals decide whether a specific behaviour is a something that is worth looking deeper into versus what is part of a normal developmental/life cycle stage, I'll describe below how this decision-making happens and what professionals primarily try to assess. Every professional is different, so I will describe what happens when someone comes to see me.

The inner workings of a psychologist

When someone initially comes to see me, my job is to understand as much as possible about their reason for being in my office. The first thing that I want to know is: what **exactly** concerns the person? If their loved ones encouraged them to attend, I want to know what

behaviours the loved ones noticed that made them worry. Details here are very important and soon you will understand why.

I also look at their intake form which lists their age and occupation. This is also very important information, as it tells me what life stage they are currently in, what stressors they are facing and potentially some insight into their personality style as well. So, for example, if a 26-year-old, self-employed tradesman is coming to see me, looking only at this information, it already tells me that he is physically active, self-motivated and focused. This person is not likely to come see me about stress regarding his Year 12 exams as he is past that developmental stage. He is more likely to be coming to see me for relationship or work concerns.

Keeping this in mind, as the person is describing to me their concerns, I also explore their lifestyle: how well are they sleeping, their eating habits, how much alcohol they consume, whether they exercise and if they use any recreational drugs. Although these questions might seem very invasive for a first meeting with someone, they are really important for me to understand the bigger picture in relation to this person. Other areas that are important to explore are: their living arrangements (who they live with), what are their hobbies and what existing emotional support they have. As you'll find out by reading this book, all aspects of the person's life are taken into an account and every bit of information that they tell me is used to understand them better in relation to the issue/s that brought them to counselling.

How do I tell whether the person's behaviour falls within or outside 'the norm'?

While the person is telling me about the potentially problematic behaviour, in my head I add up everything that they told me about

The Power of Knowledge

their lives and see how what they are doing fits, or does not fit, into their bigger picture.

I also seek information on:

- How does the behaviour impact the person and those around him/her?
- How does the behaviour impact on the person's work, relationships, hobbies, friendship and family connections?

Let's look at an example to demonstrate this. I'll exaggerate it so you can see what I mean. Let's say that a young woman, we'll call her Carrie, came into my office. Carrie reported that she loved buying shoes. In fact, she has already 400 pairs and she keeps buying them. She works full-time in fashion, earns a lot of money and can splurge on whatever she wants to. She owns an apartment and is recently single. In her opinion this is not a problem and it is her friends who worry that having 400 pairs of shoes might be looking like an obsession and they were concerned that there could be an underlying problem with Carrie.

While talking to Carrie, I noticed that she was very articulate, and indeed she was someone who cared about her appearance. She was dressed in very classy, fashionable clothes, was wearing make-up and her hair was neatly arranged in a stylish manner. She appeared to be a very positive, engaging person and when I asked what she thought about her friends' concerns, Carrie replied that she did not believe that there was anything to worry about. She explained to me that buying shoes was one of the joys in her life, aside from her family and close friends whom she also loves. On exploring whether there were other concerns, she said that perhaps she felt a bit lonely after a recent break-up, but at the same time did not feel that her life had to stop and did not feel the need for a partner. From what Carrie described to me, she sounded like an overall happy person who genuinely loved shoes, and aside from possibly compensating for a recent break-up, her life was good overall.

Back to the reason that Carrie ended up in my office: is Carrie's shoe-buying an issue for concern? What do you think?

My answer is that, taking into account all the information that she provided, I would say that buying shoes is not a problem for Carrie, and in fact it is something that is **normal for her**. In fact, had Carrie lost all interest in fashion and attended the next session wearing old, stained clothes with messy hair and did not care about her appearance, I would get concerned, as this would be out of character for her.

Similarly, if some of the details in her original story were different, the exact same behaviour of buying 400 pairs of shoes could have been seen as more problematic. For example, if Carrie reported that her buying habits had put her in large amounts of debt, or that her house is so packed with shoes that she had nowhere to sleep, then **the exact same behaviour** would have become a problem. Can you see how exactly the same behaviour could be perceived to be excessive or normal, depending on the context?

Now, there are behaviours that **irrespective of the context** must be addressed by a professional. These include:

The Power of Knowledge

- Extreme changes in behaviour:
    - changes in eating and sleeping patterns, e.g., sleeping too much or not at all; eating too much, or excessively restricting food intake
    - changes in personal hygiene or appearance
    - withdrawal from family or friends
    - withdrawal from activities that the person used to enjoy
- Suicidal ideation
- Suicidal attempts
- Threats, or thoughts about wanting to kill others (pets or humans)
- Self-harming behaviour, such as intentionally cutting oneself, burning oneself.
- Hearing, seeing, or experiencing with other senses things that are not there, especially if what the person is experiencing frightens them (e.g., voices that tell them to harm themselves or others).
- Regular angry outbursts that the person seemingly cannot control, including yelling/shouting, intimidating others, punching walls, breaking items (even if there is no one around).
- Extreme mood swings in the absence of hormonal changes or known medical conditions.

SANE Australia lists additional concerning behaviours under their factsheet 'Is someone you know unwell' – www.sane.org/information-stories/facts-and-guides/is-someone-you-know-unwell.

If the above behaviours/thoughts persist for over two weeks, they need to be discussed with a professional. Please do not delay seeking help if you recognise yourself or someone else on this list. Please note that will **not** get better on its own. It will **not** get better as time passes by. Pause the rest of the chapter, go straight to the **Additional Recommendations** sections and look up the organisation that matches the assistance that you require. If you are outside of Australia, you can still access the websites of the Australian pages. Many provide online support and may be able to direct you to similar services in your country of residence.

Degrees of severity of the behaviour

The examples above are black and white. However, in many real-life situations, the answer is not quite clear. The reason for this is because even professionals who speak to you are assessing in their minds the **degree** to which the behaviour, feeling or whatever else that concerns you is present in your life.

Many people think that psychological phenomena or psychological conditions are **categorical** – that you either have it or you don't.

For example, people might think that they either:

- Feel depressed or they don't
- Feel anxious in social situations or they don't
- Have energy in the mornings or they don't
- Get really angry when their kids push their buttons or they don't

In reality, all of this exists on a continuum, an imaginary line. Some things are more stable, such as your personality traits when you are an adult, whereas your energy can fluctuate multiple times during the day. Yet, your personality traits and your energy levels are dimensional – they fall somewhere along the continuum.

The Power of Knowledge

For example, on the line of extroversion, you could be more extroverted with close friends, but less extroverted at a work meeting. The extent to which someone expresses their extroversion may depend on many other factors, such as who is with them, how much sleep they got that night and what other stressors are happening in their lives.

Extroversion

Low   **High**

If we were in a large room with many random people and I drew a line on the floor that represented extroversion, I could ask people to stand somewhere on the line that represented their levels of extroversion in different situations. People would start to spread across that line. Some would stand near the ends, while others would be somewhere in the middle.

Let's say a person decided to come to a mental health professional, and stated that their level of extroversion was a problem for them. A mental health professional would ask for more specific information, such as:

- In what specific situations is the level of extroversion a problem?
- What other areas of life does it impact: work, relationships, hobbies, friendships or family connections?
- What else is happening for this person in the broader context? Are there cultural and gender factors and expectations that the therapist needs to take into account? For example, in some cultures extroversion is celebrated and in others less so.

In other words: Is this really a problem? Who is this a problem for?

As we saw with Carrie, buying 400 pairs of shoes concerned Carrie's friends, but it was not a problem for Carrie. In other situations, a certain behaviour can indeed be a problem, which is where the professional's role begins.

Do I really need help? Is it really *that* bad?

As a general rule, if the thought, *'Perhaps I should talk to someone about this?'* entered your mind, then please do talk to someone about it. An ethical professional will not start you on any course of treatment or therapy if it is not required. When things are challenging it is difficult to be objective with ourselves. Let a professional tell you if it's *'really that bad.'*

Where would I find the right psychologist?

The following chapters will take you through this process in detail.

This is all well and good, but what about the cost of seeing a professional?

Yes, seeing any professional costs money. If financial concerns are stopping you from seeing a mental health professional, you have a number of options:

1. Many professionals offer reduced fees for people who are unemployed or in a difficult financial situation. This

information will be on their website, or you can find it out by directly contacting the professional, discussing your situation with them and seeing whether a reduced fee can be negotiated.
2. Check whether your government runs programs that assist with the cost of seeing a mental health professional. In Australia, for example, we have the Better Outcomes in Mental Health Scheme which offers partial subsidies for psychological sessions. I will mention it in the next chapter as well. Your country may have similar programs.
3. If you notice that paying for the sessions becomes difficult once you have started your treatment, talk about this with the professional. In addition to a potential discounted fee, you may also decide to extend the time between sessions and complete homework during those gaps, so that you still maintain gains between the sessions.
4. There are a lot of good quality free programs and free online counselling available, as well as self-help books and websites that offer practical assistance. As you continue reading on this book, you will find a range of these resources listed at the end of chapters.

SUMMARY

In this chapter, we started to explore what aspects of your own or someone else's behaviour could be indicators that professional input would be helpful. I outlined behaviours that are absolute red flags of assistance being necessary, but there are many behaviours that could play on your mind and you may like to talk to someone about. Below are details of services that operate 24/7 and offer both phone and online assistance. These are Australian organisations, but if you're outside of Australia you can still access their assistance online.

CONTACT DETAILS FOR SUPPORT SERVICES:

Domestic Violence – 1800 RESPECT: Confidential support and information for people experiencing violence and abuse. Support is available online and over the phone. www.1800respect.org.au; 1800 737 732.

Mensline: Free professional 24/7 telephone and online counselling support for men concerned about mental health, anger management, family violence (using and experiencing), addiction, relationship, stress and wellbeing. www.mensline.org.au; 1300 78 99 78.

Headspace Australia: Assistance for young people aged 12-25, on topics such as: general mental health, physical health, work and study, alcohol and other drugs. They provide online and phone counselling, information and support. www.headspace.org.au; 1800 650 890.

Suicide Call Back Service: Free 24/7 counselling for suicide prevention and mental health via telephone, online and video for anyone affected by suicidal thoughts. www.suicidecallbackservice.org.au; 1300 659 467.

Kids Helpline: Free webchat and phone counselling for kids, teens, young adults, parents and carers and schools for any reason. www.kidshelpline.com.au; 1800 55 1800.

Family drug help – Family Drug and Gambling Helpline: Provides practical help, information and support to families and friends affected by drinking, drug use or gambling. Based in Victoria, Australia, the helpline operates 24/7 on 1300 660 068. www.sharc.org.au.

Anxiety support – Anxiety Recovery Centre of Victoria (ARCVic): Information, parent support, support groups, an OCD & Anxiety Helpline & Webchat – for support, information and referral; professional development.
1300 269 438 or (03) 9830 0533; www.arcvic.org.au.

Eating disorders – The Butterfly Foundation: Support for eating disorders and body image issues, including information on finding professional support for eating and body concerns. The helpline offers confidential discussion via an online chat. www.butterfly.org.au; 1800 33 4673.

SANE Australia: Information and referral on mental illness, a free counselling service available via phone, web chat or e-mail: https://www.sane.org; 1800 18 7263. Under the tab 'Factsheets and Guides', then 'Mental Health Issues', look for the factsheets on 'facts vs myths' to dispel myths surrounding mental illness.

References

Aamond, S., & Wang, S. (2012). *Welcome to Your Child's Brain: How the Mind Grows from Conception to College.* Bloomsbury.

Arain, M., Haque, M., Johal, L., Mathur, P., Nel, W., Rais, A., Sandhu, R., Sharma, S. (2013). Maturation of the Adolescent Brain. *Neuropsychiatric Disease and Treatment, 9,* 449-461. doi: 10.2147/NDT.S39776

Chapter 4

The Power of Decision-Making

'In any moment of decision, the best thing you can do is the right thing, the next best thing is the wrong thing and the worst thing you can do is nothing.'

— Theodore Roosevelt

In the previous chapter, we identified a few markers that you can use to decide whether you need to speak to someone outside your family and friendship group about what you have noticed and what concerns you. If you contacted the organisations listed on the previous page, then hopefully you already have some clarity. For those who are yet to speak to someone, this chapter will answer the question: where do I start?

What's Normal Anyway

Where do I start?

The answer is actually straightforward. If you have any concerns about your psychological wellbeing, the first professional to talk to is with your family doctor, or a general practitioner (GP) with whom you feel comfortable.

If you are still at school, then start by talking to a trusted adult: a parent, older sibling, teacher, school principal, or school welfare officer/counsellor. You will potentially still be directed to a GP, but start with what is most accessible to you where you are now.

For adult readers, there are a number of reasons why I recommend that you start by seeing a GP first:

1. There are physical conditions that can mimic the symptoms of a mental illness. Thyroid problems, a hormonal imbalance and low iron levels are conditions that can all mimic symptoms of anxiety or depression. It can be even simpler than that. A long time ago, I attended a lecture by a psychologist who specialised in sleep disorders. In his lecture, he described that many of his patients were diagnosed with depression for years, when in fact their underlying issue was sleep problems. As soon as the sleep problem was resolved, the person no longer met the criteria for depression.

If you think about it, it makes perfect sense. If you aren't sleeping properly, you're likely to be irritable, have low energy levels, your eating would potentially be out of balance and you might feel down and hopeless if your situation has not improved. These descriptions indeed resemble symptoms of depression.

Anxiety also has a physiological component to it: a racing heart, sweating, feeling light-headed and nauseous, muscle tension, tight jaws, for example. However, other medical conditions share similar symptoms. Moreover, negative lifestyle factors, such as skipping meals, not drinking enough water and high levels of stress would result in the same symptoms of anxiety.

Thus, seeing a doctor is the first step when you're not feeling quite yourself and it is to eliminate any potential underlying physical issues that could be contributing to how you are feeling. We all go through periods of stress when our sleep, diet and exercise are not prioritised. I am a big advocate of ensuring that basic physical checks (like a blood test) are done in the first instance.

2. GPs are the gatekeepers to many essential services, including mental health services. In Australia, most GPs work closely with psychologists and psychiatrists. In fact, many psychologists are based in medical centres or hospitals for this exact reason. For the past decade, I have been based in numerous medical centres, which has made it very convenient for me, for my clients and for the doctors. I could make urgent appointments for my clients with a GP when this was required, and GPs often came into my room to quickly consult regarding a patient. This collaboration is invaluable to ensure consistent patient care.

Indeed, research on successful outcomes in mental health indicates that the best outcomes in mental health are achieved through a **combination of treatments and supports**. The most common combination is medication, therapy and community support (e.g., support groups). However, different combinations work for different people. Your local doctor will be your gateway and access point to psychologists who collaborate with them, as well as a range of other services that could be helpful in navigating what you are going through.

3. Depending on where you live, you might need a referral from a GP to see a mental health professional. In Australia, **you don't have**

to have a GP's referral to see a psychologist or a social worker, but getting a referral means that you will be eligible for services that are partially subsidised by Medicare under the Better Outcomes in Mental Health Care initiative, making therapy more affordable.

Those who decide to go down that path would need to make a double appointment with their GP. The GP will then create a Mental Health Treatment Plan (MHTP).

The patient can decide who they would like to see, or the GP can make a suggestion. Your consent to get the MHTP gives the practitioner permission to communicate with your doctor about your progress in therapy, thereby facilitating better treatment outcomes.

Common concerns

I don't have a GP or I don't trust my GP

If either of the above applies to you, you have a number of options:

1. Ask trusted friends or relatives for GP recommendations. You can also use social media community groups to ask for recommendations.
2. Google doctors in your local area and read reviews. Picking a doctor who works close to your home is ideal, as the psychologists and other professionals they will recommend are also likely to be locally based, saving you the time in travelling to far away parts of your city.
3. In Australia, we have a national service called Beyond Blue that lists GPs and other mental health professionals. You can find Beyond Blue's details at the end of this chapter.

The Power of Decision-Making

I am embarrassed to speak to a doctor

This is a concern that definitely comes up, especially if there is a religious, cultural or gender taboo in relation to discussing psychological concerns.

Going to a doctor sometimes carries a connotation that you cannot solve your problems yourself. Many of us are usually capable problem-solvers and let's face it: we usually don't want to go and see a doctor unless it is absolutely necessary! Many of us wait until either the physical or the emotional pain is unbearable or until someone, like a loved one, pushes us because *they* can see that what we are going through is too much.

There's no judgement here from me. I am exactly the same. I'll tell a quick story in honour of my GP to demonstrate my point. Sometime in 2016, I accidentally dropped a glass clock on the floor and the glass deeply cut my pinky finger. I was scared and in a lot of pain. My sister was nearby and encouraged me to see a pharmacist, but I was in so much pain and wrapped the finger so tightly that I couldn't imagine anyone even breathing in its direction. A week passed and eventually I went to see my GP. The only reason I wanted to see him was to ensure that the finger was healing well. I was so ashamed of this incident. My GP was unhappy that I left my visit for so long. I have three degrees in psychology! He expected me to know better. In his typical humorous way, he figuratively speaking slapped me on the head and then examined the finger. It was clean and had already healed. He determined that the nerves were working and said that if it was another millimetre, I would have damaged a nerve and he'd be referring me to a specialist.

What's Normal Anyway

The lessons to be learned from this story are:

- Psychologists are people too, and even with many degrees, we aren't immune to emotions or feelings of inadequacy and fear.
- We are all proud, we all want to feel that we are own experts, our own specialists and we can solve everything on our own. Yet, there are people who have dedicated their entire lives to medicine or psychology or any other specialty field. We can't compete with their years of study and training. In one glance, my GP gave me a full trajectory of what could've been. That's the result of decades of study and work experience in his chosen field.

I still feel anxiety and resistance about seeing a GP or another specialist and still not as quick to raise my hand when I need help, but I remind myself that a doctor is a professional. That they have seen and heard everything probably a million times before and ultimately the reason that they decided to spend years of their lives doing medicine is because they want to help others.

'A problem shared is a problem halved.'
 — **English Proverb**

So, I would encourage you to take a deep breath, acknowledge that seeing a doctor and indeed any specialist can be scary, uncomfortable, uncertain, embarrassing, anxiety-provoking and yet – sometimes it still has to be done.

If you do decide to see a doctor after all, here are a few suggestions:

1. Start talking to your GP even if you have no current concerns about your mental health. Get to know them so that when you need support in future, you can trust their input.

2. Bring a friend or a family member along to the first appointment until you are more comfortable with your doctor.
3. If you believe that a doctor from your own cultural background and who speaks your native language is going to make the process more comfortable for you, make an appointment with them.
4. If you're concerned that there will be unpleasant repercussions for you after seeing a doctor in your community (e.g., you'll be dreading bumping into the doctor at the supermarket), see a GP outside your community.
5. Consider whether you'd be more comfortable speaking about your concerns with a male or a female GP? Younger or older? My older male clients are often uncomfortable talking to me about relationship problems. They prefer to be referred to an older male therapist to discuss these types of concerns.

I am anxious about what the doctor will say

> *'Fear keeps us focused on the past or worried about the future. If we can acknowledge our fear, we can realize that right now we are okay.'*
>
> **– Thich Nhat Hanh**

In our heads, our thoughts seem a lot messier and more catastrophic than what a trained professional would make out of them. You might be imagining the absolute worst-case scenario, like: *'They will think that I'm crazy,'* or, *'What if they send me to a mental institution?'* However, your GP is trained to view information through clinical eyes, and they'll be asking only what's necessary for them to decide on the next step.

In terms of psychiatric facilities, a person needs to meet a very specific criteria to get into a psychiatric hospital. Even in developed countries, there is a shortage of beds, staff and funding issues. Psychiatric facilities are also now part of hospitals and offer a modern, holistic approach to recovery. Still, as my supervisor stated, *'Psychiatric institutions are the last stop towards stabilisation'*. Thus, your first meeting with a GP about psychological concerns is most likely going to focus on getting you support within the community, such a referral to a local psychologist. SANE Australia has fantastic information to dispel common myths about mental illness, which I have added to the resource section of this chapter.

What will the GP ask me?

The GP is likely to want details about what you have noticed, what concerns you and how long it has been going on for. It may be a good idea for you to write down a few bullet points to ensure you tell the doctor all the relevant information. Everything that you describe will help the doctor guide further questions and decide on an appropriate referral, if it is required.

SUMMARY

In this chapter, we looked at the first step that you need to take if you wish to access psychological help. For those still at school, the first step is to talk to a trusted adult, such as a parent, teacher or your school's welfare coordinator. For adults, the first step is to see a GP. We also went over common obstacles and anxieties that can arise prior to the visit and tips for overcoming them.

In the next chapter, we will explore in more depth the mental health professionals that your GP can refer you to and what will guide this decision.

The Power of Decision-Making

Further information

- **Beyond Blue's** website includes extensive information on support services, online support and provides a list of GPs and mental health professionals in Australia: www.beyondblue.org.au/get-support/find-a-professional, 1300 22 4636.

- **SANE Australia** – www.sane.org. Under the tab 'Factsheets and Guides' and 'Mental Health Issues' look for the factsheets on 'facts vs myth' to dispel myths on mental illness.

- **Better Health Channel** offers a good summary on how to seek help for a psychological concern: www.betterhealth.vic.gov.au/health/conditionsandtreatments/mental-illness-treatments

Chapter 5

The Power of Discernment

'The most difficult thing is the decision to act, the rest is merely tenacity.'

– Amelia Earhart

In the previous chapter, we discussed overcoming your concerns and anxieties about seeing a GP. In this chapter, we will look at who the GP can refer you to in relation to any psychological concerns you are experiencing, and the differences between the different professionals. I will outline the differences between the most common mental health professionals, focusing especially on the ones whom your GP is likely to refer you to.

Why is this important?

1. Knowing your options gives you greater control

In this day and age, there are many people who feel called to help others. This is fantastic, as it gives a lot of options for those seeking help. However, with so much information out there and all the different titles, it can get confusing.

> **Here is a sample of the most common different titles for professionals who deal with psychological concerns, or are in the field of self-development:**
>
> • Counsellor • Psychologist • Psychiatrist • Support worker
>
> • Psychotherapist • Social worker • Hypnotherapist • Youth worker
>
> • Therapist • Mental health nurse • Case manager • Life coach

This list is not exhaustive, but it is no wonder that people get confused. Is there any difference between these professionals? Would there be any substantial difference in a person's treatment outcomes if they see one and not the other? How would a person even find them?

As one of my mentors often says, '*A confused mind always says no,*' and with this list, it is easy to see why many people give up on seeking help when presented with so many different choices and no clear explanation about these titles.

The Power of Discernment

2. Knowing who you will see will help you to match your expectations to what the professional can offer

This is a basic principle. The person you are seeing needs to be able to assist with your concern, otherwise it is a waste of time for both of you. You wouldn't attend a dental appointment expecting to get an assessment of your eyesight, right?

I cannot tell you how many times, as soon as I told someone that I was a psychologist, they had an expectation that:

- **I will read their thoughts and predict their future.** This can at times be fun, especially when the person follows with, *'I'm not saying another word next to you,'* and hurriedly escapes before I put my mind-reading skills into action and announce to the world their deepest thoughts. Alas, I can't read minds, but they rarely stick around to find that out.
- **I will tell them everything about their personality traits just by looking at them.** Then some people actually waited for me to impress them with my in-depth analysis of their entire being. Completing a personality test would make the task more manageable.
- **I will recommend the best antidepressant for them.** This happens frequently. As I am not a medical doctor, I cannot prescribe medication and so I leave this area for their doctor to comment on.
- **The clients will be lying on a couch and I will sit by their side and analyse their dreams.** Firstly, not all psychologists conduct counselling sessions or see clients. There are many branches of psychology and many jobs that psychologists can do. Some psychologists, for example, become academics, and their work involves research, teaching or supervision of students in academic institutions. Other psychologists

specialise in working with organisations rather than individuals. Thus, just because someone is a psychologist, it does not automatically follow that they are counselling clients.

Those psychologists who do counselling work with clients often have couches, chairs or armchairs in their offices. However, most clients sit on the couch and are facing the therapist. In terms of dream analysis, I can speak for myself that my psychology training definitely did not include this in the curriculum. Thus, if clients attend a session, hoping that I'll be able to interpret their dreams, they'll be disappointed.

I am sure that many of my colleagues had experienced at least some of the above comments or expectations at some point. It is funny in some situations, but people actually do book appointments, wait a few weeks or even months, then attend a session with a particular mental health specialist expecting something that the professional cannot provide. So, it is definitely worthwhile to at least have a basic idea of what to expect from which mental health professional. This will save you money, time and help protect you from disappointment due to mismatched expectations.

3. There are differences in the specialised training of mental health professionals. This can have implications for their level of responsibility towards the public.

As a general rule, the more specialised a professional's training, the higher their level of responsibility to the consumer and the more responsibility the professional has to follow ethical and code of practice requirements. This is important to know if you want to see a professional whose field of work is regulated, versus someone who is perhaps incredible at what they do, but they don't have a formal qualification.

The Power of Discernment

What is a regulated industry?

According to the Cambridge Business English Dictionary, a regulated industry is: *'A type of business that is controlled by government rules'* (www.dictionary.cambridge.org). In regulated industries certain standards are decided on that will protect the consumer from being harmed or taken advantage of. Those who decide to work in those regulated industries must meet certain standards and there are serious legal implications for any breaches.

In a FindLaw blog post, Ephrat Livni notes: *'The most regulated industries are those which have the deepest impact on people's lives and could cause the most potential harm. So, it should probably come as no surprise that healthcare is the most regulated industry of them all'* (Livni, 2016).

Regulation bodies are set up with the primary aim of protecting the public from harm by setting policies and standards of care, overseeing training of medical professionals (starting from courses that meet the board's set criteria, to examinations and tests that students must pass), training of supervisors and ongoing monitoring to make sure that industry standards are met.

In Australia, the Australian Health Practitioner Regulation Agency (AHPRA) works with 15 National Boards, including the Psychology Board of Australia and Medical Board of Australia. Every year registered practitioners must meet criteria such as recency of practice and continued professional development. This means that even after someone has finished their formal studies and training, they must continue to receive regular supervision from their peers and/or senior practitioners to ensure that their work is of a high ethical and professional standard; they must complete a certain number of hours of additional learning each year; and they are expected to work within their area of competency/expertise. Psychologists, for example, must complete at least 30 hours of continued professional development of which at least 10 hours are under direct supervision. Thus, during the year, my colleagues and I attend regular workshops, seminars, webinars and meet with one another to discuss any challenges or difficulties. Psychiatrists and GPs are required to complete at least 50 hours of professional development a year (www.ranzcp.org; www.ahpra.gov.au).

Psychologists, psychiatrists, GPs, nurses, pharmacists, dentists and other professionals must be registered with AHPRA to work in Australia. In other countries there are different names for registration boards and different rules to receive full registration, but the aim is the same: to protect the public from harm. It is highly likely that in your country, psychologists and psychiatrists are regulated. Of course, not everyone acts 'by the book' and this is where the registration board comes into play: professionals can be deregistered if they are found to be in breach of rules and regulations. Indeed, the registration boards list those professionals who are found to be in breach of conduct.

Unregulated healthcare industries

There are health professionals whose industries are not formally regulated, and in the next section we will describe a number of these industries in the context of seeking psychological support.

Please bear in mind that you are free to choose who you wish to work with. An important point to be mindful of is that when you see a mental health professional, whether their industry is regulated or not, there is **an imbalance of power between you and the professional.** No matter how lovely the professional is, no matter how much they may genuinely wish for the relationship to be 'equal', to remove the separation between you and them and for you not to put them on a pedestal, since this is a professional relationship, the person you are seeing holds the power. You are seeing them because you believe that they can assist you in some way. Therefore, you put your trust in them. Thus, they have the authority to act. Their words have more weight than those of your best friend and their recommendations carry more meaning than your grandmother's recommendations. This is true for any professional. When seeking support for mental health, I believe it is even more important to take great care who you disclose personal information to as we are often in a vulnerable emotional state when we seek help for psychological concerns.

More qualified does not necessarily mean better

Having said that, there are still, of course, individual differences between professionals. Someone could be an academic genius in their field of psychiatry, but this does not mean that you'll connect with them on a personal level. Yet another person could be someone did not finish high school but decided to become a life coach, and their words and wisdom resonate with you. Find someone you can connect to and also be aware of who you are seeing, what obligations and responsibilities they have towards you and who holds them accountable to ensure that they meet those obligations.

Meet the team:

Psychiatrists

The Royal Australian and New Zealand College of Psychiatrists (RANZCP) provided the following definition of psychiatrists: *'A psychiatrist is a specialist medical doctor who assesses and treats patients with mental health problems. He or she is skilled in undertaking a comprehensive psychiatric assessment to arrive at an accurate diagnosis and formulation that considers the interaction between physical and mental illness and the unique needs and attributes of the individual patient.'* (RANZCP, 2013, para. 3).

At the end of this chapter, you will find the full reference to the article by RANZCP from which I have taken the above quote. I would strongly encourage you to read the article in full, as it describes in great detail the role and responsibilities of psychiatrists.

To summarise the information, psychiatrists are, first and foremost, **medical professionals** who chose to undertake additional training in the area of mental health, just as there are doctors who decided to specialise in neurology, cardiology, gynaecology or any other branch of medicine.

Since psychiatrists are specialist doctors, the only way to see a psychiatrist in Australia is through a referral from your GP, just like if you needed to see a specialist for any other part of your body. So, if your GP decided that a referral to a psychiatrist was necessary, it did not mean that they thought you were 'crazy'. Rather, it meant that they recognised that a specialist input was required in order to provide you with the most comprehensive health care. It is part of a GP's job and duty of care to ensure that their patients receive the best treatment for their needs. Therefore, when appropriate, this can involve a referral to a specialist mental health practitioner.

Breaking the stigma of seeing a psychiatrist

I once had a very memorable client. He was a practical, professional man in his late 50s who felt anxious at work. His workplace was demanding, and the pressure was taking its toll. Coming to see me was

The Power of Discernment

a big step for him, and he had high hopes that talking therapy would improve the situation. However, after about two months of regular sessions, little progress was made. I had a discussion with my client about additional options and in this case, I recommended a referral to a psychiatrist as I felt that this case required more specialised input. Very often, psychologists work with multiple professionals, as every professional brings their training and expertise to the table.

Whilst I was excited about the prospect of my client receiving specialised input from a psychiatrist, my client didn't want to hear about it. They claimed that seeing a psychiatrist meant that they were more unwell than they believed to be and that it was an unnecessary 'escalation' of a situation. Although I disagreed with their interpretation, I also understood their fear, so we continued with only the talking therapy.

> *'Doing the same thing over and over again and expecting different results when, in fact, the results never change, is one definition of insanity.'*
>
> **– Lawrence Kudlow**

My client was not insane; he was scared of the unknown. However, as we changed nothing, nothing changed. With pressure at work increasing, my client eventually agreed to see a psychiatrist. With my client's permission, I spoke to the psychiatrist to provide information on what I observed in the sessions and to hear their perspective on what could work. As a team that consisted of the client, GP, psychiatrist and myself (a psychologist), we agreed on a treatment plan. As part of that treatment plan, my client started on a course of psychotropic medications and the difference in his presentation in our sessions was almost immediate. My client was less anxious, his thoughts were not racing as much, he was able to engage in sessions better, and even his work colleagues were commenting on the improvements in his demeanour.

My client was also referred to attend a therapy group through the psychiatric hospital where their new psychiatrist worked. Even though the stigma of attending a psychiatric hospital frightened my client, he was surprised at how much he enjoyed these groups. Do you know why? Because, for the first time in many years, he met other people who shared similar fears and concerns! My client felt less alone by attending the group. His experiences were normalised, not only by the medical team, but also by other 'ordinary' people. You may remember from the previous chapters how important social support can be.

Many of us are scared of what we don't understand, which is why it is so important to have at least a GP whose opinion you trust. In my client's case, the course of action recommended by his medical team was the right step forward. My client no longer viewed seeing a psychiatrist and attending group treatment as something shameful, but rather as an investment in his health.

Fear of taking psychotropic medications

Similar to the stigma of seeing a psychiatrist or psychologist, there is a stigma associated with taking medications for psychological conditions. Once again, the impression might be as if taking these medications indicates that the person is 'crazy', or that they are so unwell that they cannot solve the issue by themselves. However, how would you look at someone if you learned that they were taking medication for their blood pressure? Would that make you feel uncomfortable, or perhaps lead you to think that this person was 'inept' at regulating their own blood pressure?

The Power of Discernment

From what I have observed, we display a much more forgiving and compassionate attitude when it comes to taking medication for non-psychological conditions.

Most of my clients do not require psychotropic medications. However, those who are recommended medications are initially frightened and disappointed. Many of them worry about the side effects and the fact that this may be for the rest of their lives. They feel a sense of failure.

However, at least in my professional experience, their fears do not eventuate. My clients who have been recommended psychotropic medications by their GPs or their psychiatrists report significant and noticeable improvements in their mood, in the clarity of their thinking and in their capacity to concentrate. Yes, it was an adjustment for some to start taking medication, and in addition to their own feelings of perceived defeat and failure, they at times also cope with other people's stigma. They had to change their behaviours, such as drinking non-alcoholic beer at parties so they could still participate in festivities without reducing the effectiveness of the medications.

This is not dissimilar to a person with a diagnosis of diabetes who needed to change their lifestyle habits and take medications in order to manage their condition. Not every person with a psychological condition will require medication, but there are cases where talking therapy alone is not enough and additional treatments need to be considered. When you have a trusted professional, or a team of professionals, it makes it easier to openly discuss your fears and concerns. SANE Australia (www.sane.org) covers this topic well in their factsheets and guides on the topic of 'Treatments for mental health issues'.

Psychologists

Psychologists are mental health professionals who have completed at least four years of university training, plus years of supervised practice. Psychologists are not doctors and **cannot prescribe medications**. They provide talking therapies, and their profession is regulated by the local and national bodies. The title 'psychologist' is regulated and restricted to the profession. This means that only individuals who have completed all the requirements prescribed by their regulatory body can use this title. Furthermore, there are psychologists who have completed additional training and specialisation and they can add their specialisation to their title. Thus, if you see titles such as a 'Clinical Psychologist', 'Counselling Psychologist', 'Forensic Psychologist', 'Organisational Psychologist', for example, this means that the professional has completed additional years of training and supervision to attain this specialisation.

Social workers

Social workers receive broader education than psychologists and complete at least three years of university training. In Australia, the social work profession is self-regulated. To cite Cindy Smith, the chief executive of the professional body of social workers in Australia, the Australian Association of Social Workers (AASW):

'Unfortunately, at the moment there are no mechanisms to prevent someone from calling themselves a social worker when they do not actually hold a social worker qualification. Social work is not a registered profession and this is something that must change' (as cited in AASW's media release, 9 June 2021).

Thus, social workers are currently not registered with the Australian Health Practitioner Regulation Agency. However, by registering with AASW, *'Social workers can distinguish themselves to clients, employers and the general public as professionals with legitimate credentials'* (AASW) and are bound by the practice standards and the Code of Ethics that the AASW developed. There are also Accredited Mental Health Social Workers (AMHSW), who have additional training in mental health. Social workers who are registered with AASW can be searched on their register, at www.aasw.asn.au. Like psychologists and psychiatrists, social workers can choose to specialise in particular areas of mental health, such as relationship counselling, trauma or drugs and alcohol.

Counsellors, therapists and psychotherapists

'There is no law in Australia that requires a person who provides a counselling service to have either qualifications or experience. This means that people without training or skills can call themselves counsellors or psychotherapists' (Australia. Better Health Channel, 2019).

There are organisations in Australia that offer certificates, diplomas and even master's degrees in the areas of counselling and psychotherapy, and practitioners can choose whether to register with those organisations. Two peak bodies in Australia that provide national standards for counsellors and psychotherapists are the Australian Counselling Association (ACA) and the Psychotherapy and Counselling Federation of Australia (PACFA). If you live in Australia and decide to see any of the above professionals, you can check whether the person you wish to see is registered with these organisations. If you live outside of Australia, look up whether there are professional bodies for counsellors and psychotherapists in your country/area.

The word 'therapist' is a general word that anyone can use. You'll notice that in this book I use the word 'therapist' and 'psychologist' interchangeably. This is mainly for convenience and to cover therapists who are not psychologists.

Life coaches, personal coaches, holistic health coaches and mentors

According to the *Legal Guide for Life Coaches, Business Coaches and Mentors* (Emilio, 2021), in Australia, anyone can call themselves any of the above titles. Coaches who wish to distinguish themselves as trained professionals can complete courses and graduate from accredited coaching programs.

The *Legal Guide for Life Coaches, Business Coaches and Mentors* lists *'two major international organisations that offer accreditation of coaching programs'*:

- International Coach Federation (ICF – Australasia)
- International Association of Coaching

This list is potentially non-exhaustive, but I hope that you are starting to get the idea that irrespective of who you decide to see, make sure that you check the person's qualifications and credentials and whether they are a member of their respective professional body.

Specialties

Often professionals decide to specialise in a particular area of interest. This means that above and beyond their base training, they decided to undertake additional training in one or more speciality areas which include:

The Power of Discernment

- Anxiety disorders
- Workplace issues
- Domestic violence
- Men's issues
- Trauma work
- Suicide prevention
- Children and adolescents
- Gambling and other addictions
- Drugs and alcohol
- Eating disorders
- Women's issues
- Grief and loss
- Family work
- Relationships
- Sleeping disorders
- Bipolar disorder
- Psychotic illnesses
- LGBTQ support

There are psychiatrists, psychologists, social workers, counsellors and therapists who specialise in the above categories. There are also general psychology practitioners, like myself – I'm a general psychologist, so I manage and treat psychological conditions. If someone comes to see me and their concern is of a specialised nature (like an eating disorder or couples counselling), I refer them to services and professionals who specialise in the area.

How do I decide who to see?

1. Decide on your primary concern: are you concerned about yourself or someone else?
2. What broad issue does your concern fall into? In what area is the biggest struggle?
3. Decide on the level of training/education of the person who you'd like to see to narrow the field. If the person is a psychologist, social worker or psychiatrist, then a GP can refer you to the appropriate one for your needs.
4. You could look up the professionals in your local area who have the particular specialisation you are looking for. If you are considering a particular person, have a look at their online profile or directly ask them about their qualifications and specialty area/s. This will increase the chances of you booking an appointment with someone who matches your expectations.

5. Ring organisations in your area that specialise in that field and see if they can make a recommendation.

The recommendations from the previous chapter in terms of a GP's gender, age and cultural background also apply to finding the right therapist for you:

- Consider if you are more comfortable seeing a male, female or non-binary practitioner. Depending on your concerns, the therapist's gender may or may not make a difference.
- Your cultural background and upbringing could play a role in your choice of a therapist. If you believe that a therapist from your own cultural background and who speaks your native language is going to make the process more comfortable for you, then this would also be a factor in choosing a therapist. We live in a multicultural world. Not everyone speaks fluent English or is able to express themselves fluently in English. There are, however, a number of options, including engaging an interpreter.
- Age is another factor to consider. Would you like to see someone who is older or younger than you? I would encourage you to keep an open mind. Age does not necessarily mean a wealth of experience. The field of mental health can be a bit deceiving from that perspective. A brand new student of counselling could be in his late 50s with a lot of personal experience but still training up his or her skills. Or it could be a woman in her mid-20s who has been doing self-development work for the last decade. Don't judge a therapist by age alone. Have at least two sessions with them to ascertain if they are the right person for you.

SUMMARY

In this chapter, I introduced different mental health professionals: how they differ from one another in terms of their levels of education and how strictly their industries are regulated. We also looked at the broad areas of interest that these professionals have and how to decide on the right professional for you.

Additional information

- For more information on the differences between psychiatrists and psychologists, visit: https://www.healthdirect.gov.au/psychiatrists-vs-psychologists

- For detailed information on the role of psychiatrists and their responsibilities in Australia and New Zealand, visit: www.ranzcp.org/news-policy/policy-and-advocacy/position-statements/role-of-psychiatrist-in-australia-and-new-zealand

- For further information on treatments for mental health issues, visit SANE Australia on: www.sane.org/information-stories/facts-and-guides/treatments-for-mental-illness

- **ACA** – Australian Counselling Association: the premier peak body for counsellors and psychotherapists in Australia. You can find a registered counsellor on www.theaca.net.au; 1300 784 333.

- **AASW** – Australian Association of Social Workers: the professional representative body of social workers in Australia. Find a social worker on www.aasw.asn.au; 1800 630 124.

- **AHPRA** – Australian Health Regulation Practitioner Registry, where you can check that your practitioner is registered in Australia. www.ahpra.gov.au; 1300 419 495.

References

Australia. Australian Association of Social Workers (9 June, 2021). *Social workers registration is essential in Australia.* http://www.aasw.asn.au/news-media/2021/social-worker-registration-is-essential-in-australia.

Australia. Australian Association of Social Workers. *Recognising qualified social workers.* http://www.aasw.asn.au/information-for-the-community/recognising-qualified-social-workers.

Australia. Better Health Channel (2019). *Counsellors.* https://www.betterhealth.vic.gov.au/health/conditionsandtreatments/counsellors

Emilio, V. (2021). *Legal Guides for Life Coaches, Business Coaches and Mentors.* https://legal123.com.au/how-to-guide/legal-guide-life-coaches/

Livni, E. (2016). *Regulation Nation: What Industries Are Most Carefully Overseen?* www.findlaw.com/legalblogs/small-business/regulation-nation-what-industries-are-most-carefully-overseen.

The Royal Australian and New Zealand College of Psychiatrists. *The role of the psychiatrist in Australia and New Zealand: Position Statement 80, November 2013.* www.ranzcp.org/news-policy/policy-and-advocacy/position-statements/role-of-psychiatrist-in-australia-and-new-zealand

Chapter 6

The Power of Diversity

'Our diversity is our strength. What a dull and pointless life it would be if everyone was the same.'

– Angelina Jolie

The previous chapter gave you an overview on the variety of mental health and wellbeing professionals out there. In this chapter, I will introduce you to some of the therapies that these professionals use in their work.

Why is this important?

My aim is to give you as much information as possible within the scope of this book so you can make informed decisions that will increase your chances of attaining a successful outcome through therapy.

Certain therapies are particularly effective for certain issues

If you are seeking assistance for a specific issue, it is worthwhile to know what type of therapy it is best suited to. Every therapy that a psychologist uses in their work must be well-established. This means that the most common therapies that psychologists utilise have been researched, tested and evaluated to show that they do work. However, every therapy has its own angle and some work better for specific issues. For example, symptoms of anxiety and depression respond well to therapies such as Cognitive Behavioural Therapy (CBT) and Acceptance Commitment Therapy (ACT), which has become more prominent in the last decade or so.

Indeed, psychological therapies are constantly developing and evolving, just as the society evolves. Thus, at different times in human history, different therapies become more central. At some point Psychotherapy, Gestalt Therapy and Schema Therapy were leading the way and previous generations of psychologists were trained in these modalities. CBT then rose to glory and is still very much in use, although by the time that I studied, additional therapies were already added to our repertoire, with the focus being on short-term therapies. The current generation of psychologist trainees would be receiving training in the most current therapies, with a few prominent 'oldies' in the mix.

A relatively new intervention that has shown to be particularly effective for trauma is Eye Movement Desensitisation and Reprocessing (EMDR) therapy. The EMDR International Association (www.emdria.org), defines EMDR as *an extensively researched, effective psychotherapy method proven to help people recover from trauma and other distressing life experiences*' by using bilateral stimulation.

Having an idea of what your issue is could be the starting point to narrowing down the therapist and the type of therapy that would be most effective. Otherwise, you could end up spending months or years in therapy trying to work on an issue from an unsuitable angle.

Your personality matters

Some therapies are intended to be short-term (such as the Solution-Focused Brief Therapy) while others are intended to be long-term (such as Psychotherapy or Emotion-Focused therapies). In my experience, I have noticed that people who are outcome-driven and know exactly what they want to achieve from their sessions prefer the short-term therapies.

These kinds of personalities are often busy intellectuals who attend the session with a very specific, well-defined issue in mind and do not necessarily wish to go too far into the past and talk about their childhoods.

Someone with a dynamic, outcome-driven personality might struggle with open-ended sessions and therapists who talk a lot. They might be thinking, *'Oh, please, let's get to the point!'* and might leave these sessions very frustrated, but will feel invigorated and accomplished when walking out of a session with a therapist who uses outcome-driven therapies.

By the same token, there would be people who would absolutely love sessions where they can theorise, explore the meaning of life and philosophise on everything. These kinds of deep thinkers might feel rushed or misunderstood in the sessions with a goal-oriented therapist.

They potentially would feel more comfortable with a therapist who also enjoys deep discussions without necessarily having a 'goal' for the discussion. Why not? Everyone is different. Hurray for diversity!

A quick tip: Therapists tend to pick for themselves therapies that *they* feel most aligned with personally. If you see on a therapist's online profile that they primarily offer Psychotherapy, Gestalt therapy, Narrative Therapy or similar, then this therapist is very likely to be a person who enjoys delving deep into the psyche and talking about the meaning of things.

Therapists who enjoy the dynamic, action-taking therapies are more likely to be drawn to CBT, Solution-Focused Brief Therapy (SFBT), Acceptance Commitment Therapy (ACT) and use a combination of techniques from other therapies to achieve fast and long-lasting results. Of course, there would also be therapists who mix it up and are trained in a wide range of therapies that match their varied interests.

Don't try to fit into something that doesn't fit you

This is an important point to understand. With the variety of therapies out there, there really is no need to 'settle' for something that is not suitable to your personality or your issue. This goes for group therapies as well. If you are leaving the sessions (group or individual) feeling frustrated, annoyed and dreading going back – there is a chance that it is not the right fit for you. I always encourage people to openly discuss any such feelings with the therapist and to see what may be happening there for you.

The Power of Diversity

Types of therapy

This section introduces you to the most common therapies currently available. Please note that the list is non-exhaustive, and that depending on the person's area of training and expertise, they can utilise and combine multiple therapies in their practice.

Most therapies look at three different aspects of the person, in a variety of ways:

1. **Cognition**: Focuses on the person's thinking process, their perception of themselves and others, the conclusions that they make about themselves and others and decision-making.

2. **Emotion:** Includes both our feelings, but also the physical sensations of the feelings. For example, feeling irritated with someone and experiencing the sensations that come with irritation, including body's temperature increasing, muscles tensing and an adrenaline rush in the body.

3. **Behaviour:** The visible result of our actions, thoughts and feelings. A person who feels irritated might feel like screaming, crying, raising their voice, punching or kicking.

At the heart of it, most therapies aim to:

- Increase self-awareness
- Expand the range of ways that one can think, feel and behave
- Process challenging events in a way that helps to integrate the experience
- Allow the person to feel heard, seen and validated

What's Normal Anyway

The table below helps to give you an appreciation of some of the therapies available:

Cognitive Behavioural Therapy (CBT)	Play-Based Therapy	Motivational Interviewing	Gestalt Therapy
Solution-Focused Brief Therapy (SFBT)	Emotion-Focused Therapy (EFT)	Internal Family Systems	Couple's Therapies
Acceptance Commitment Therapy (ACT)	Dialectical Behavioural Therapy (DBT)	Interpersonal Therapy	Schema Therapy
Eye Movement Desensitisation Reprocessing (EMDR)	Psychotherapy	Narrative Therapy	Family Therapies

In the section below, I'll describe some of the therapies that I use in my practice and examples to illustrate them.

Solution-Focused Brief Therapy (SFBT): A short-term therapy that was originally designed to be used in situations when the therapist had only one or very few sessions with a person. SFBT empowers the person by helping them come up with their own solutions. This was the first therapy type that I was taught in my first year of my Master of Counselling Psychology degree. All of the students were about to start their first placements and, as the techniques of SFBT were fairly straightforward as well as effective, this was a great therapy to learn for beginning counselling students.

The Power of Diversity

It all went great for me, until I started my final placement for organisations where employees could access up to six counselling sessions. Short-term therapy was what was needed, but the issues that my clients were presenting with were at times complex. Some of the concerns included: grief-and-loss, infertility, divorce and parenting concerns, personality disorders, workplace stress and severe trauma. It was a great exposure to a range of issues for a beginning therapist, but I had limited tools in my 'therapies toolkit'.

My most shocking experience was when a client in her mid-20s attended a session with me. She reported that she was diagnosed with a personality disorder and was struggling with some matters at work. An experienced therapist immediately would've realised that six counselling sessions wouldn't cut it here, as building trust alone could take multiple sessions. However, I was armed with CBT and SFBT.

The first session went without an incident, but during the second session, the client dived fully into the multiple issues that she was experiencing. Overwhelmed, but still trying to be of help, I decided to go for one of the most common techniques of SFBT: 'The Miracle Question.' I had used this technique before with success, but on that day things went pear-shaped.

For those of you who are not familiar with this technique, 'The Miracle Question' is designed to get a person to envision a better life than they are currently living and to allow themselves to believe that things *can* get better. It is designed to elicit hope, no matter how bleak things may seem. It starts by the therapist asking the person something along the lines of:

'Imagine that tonight you will go to bed as you normally do, but while you are sleeping, a miracle is going to happen! And the miracle is that

all the things that you just mentioned, everything that had brought you to counselling, somehow, they have been resolved. However, since you are sleeping, you don't know that this had happened. Once you wake up you realise that something is different. A miracle must have happened! My question to you is: what would be the very first thing that you would notice upon waking up that would tell you that a miracle occurred?'

Usually, the person takes time to reflect on the question and then the rest of the steps of this technique are followed. Well, in the case of that client, we never went beyond the original question. As soon as I finished asking what would be the first thing that she would notice upon waking up, she almost yelled: *'I'd be a f***en billionaire! I'd wake up living in a mansion! What kind of a question is that?'*

Noticing that she is getting agitated but trusting the technique of 'The Miracle Question', which encourages to go with the client's answer – even if their miracle seems unlikely, I continued: *'Wow, OK. That would be quite a miracle. Let's go with that. So, as a billionaire waking up in the mansion, what would be the next thing that you would notice being different?'*. To my shock, the client then started wailing: *'I'm never going to be a billionaire! What's the point of answering this?',* she yelled. They didn't cover this in the textbook…

The more animated she became, the more I desperately tried to come up with something to reduce her agitation, but my attempts were unsuccessful. Within a minute or so she said: *'I'm getting a headache, can I leave?'.* Still shocked but without further ideas, I said, *'Okay,'* and silently walked her out. I returned to my room wide-eyed and speechless, trying to get my head around what had happened and pinpoint where things went wrong.

The Power of Diversity

Thankfully, I had a number of senior colleagues to discuss this with. There were many learning points to be gleaned for a beginning psychologist, mainly in reducing expectations of what can be addressed in three to six sessions and not rushing the process of therapy. 'The Miracle Question' remains an effective strategy of Solution-Focused Brief Therapy and it gives real hope to many of my clients and tangible results that keep them motivated as they are working through their concerns.

Cognitive Behavioural Therapy (CBT): Founded by Dr Aaron T. Beck in the 1960s, this therapy works with the idea that what happens to us is not as important as what we think about what happens. Using the example of the above client, I could have decided that counselling just wasn't for me and that I ruined this person's life. Instead, I took it as: *'This is an unpleasant experience, but there is a lot to learn here. I'll refer the client to a more senior clinician and will continue working on my skills.'*

CBT stipulates that the exact same event can evoke different reactions in different people. A rain for a farmer is a blessing and the exact same rain can be a disaster for a couple on their wedding day. The rain in and of itself is neither good nor bad. It just is. However, it is the *perception* of the event (the rain) that leads people to feel and act a certain way, in response to that perception. I will give an example shortly to demonstrate how this could look in the 'rain on a wedding day' scenario.

Underlying our thoughts are our core beliefs about ourselves and the world, which we have developed over time based on our life experiences. CBT focuses on challenging the negative core beliefs, as these are the beliefs that lead to distress. Some of the core beliefs could be: *'I am worthless,' 'Nobody truly cares about me,' 'If anything bad is going to happen, it will happen to me,'* or, *'I never get my way in life'.* These core beliefs impact on the person's attitude. If I believe that I am worthless and nothing ever goes my way, then what is the point in trying to improve things in my life? A CBT practitioner delves deeper into the core beliefs and unpacks them further, which is beyond the scope of this chapter. However, there are a lot of great resources available on the topic to learn more.

The webpage Psychology Tools (www.psychologytools.com) outlines a fantastic in-depth explanation of CBT principles and in its section on attitudes, it also appropriately included the famous quote by Viktor Frankl, a survivor of the Nazi concentration camps:

'Everything can be taken from a man but one thing: the last of the human freedoms – to choose one's attitude in any given set of circumstances, to choose one's own way.'

CBT encourages people to focus on what they *can* change in an upsetting or challenging situation: their thoughts, perceptions and attitudes.

Most therapists unpack CBT using triangles to show the connection between the thoughts, the feelings and the behaviours. Here is an example where the rain is perceived as a disaster:

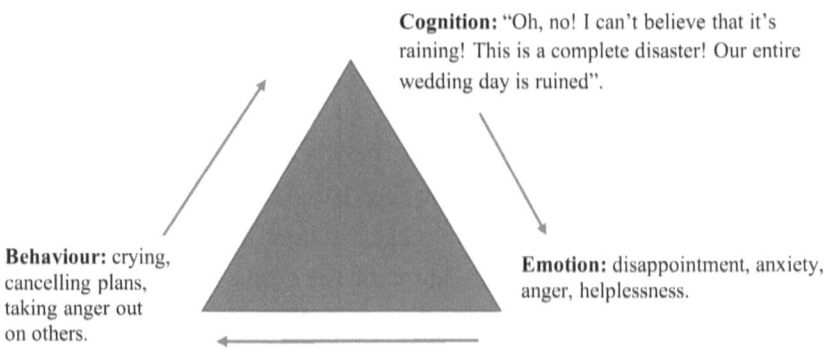

The Power of Diversity

The arrows in the diagram above can keep going around in a circle, or in reverse, creating a spiral of 'doom and gloom'. As all sections of the triangle are connected, each section impacts the other two. There are many techniques utilised through CBT and it is a well-researched therapy. One of its techniques involves finding a different way to view the exact same situation, allowing for the possibility that there is more than one way to perceive events. Taking the same example of rain on a wedding day, another way of viewing the situation could be:

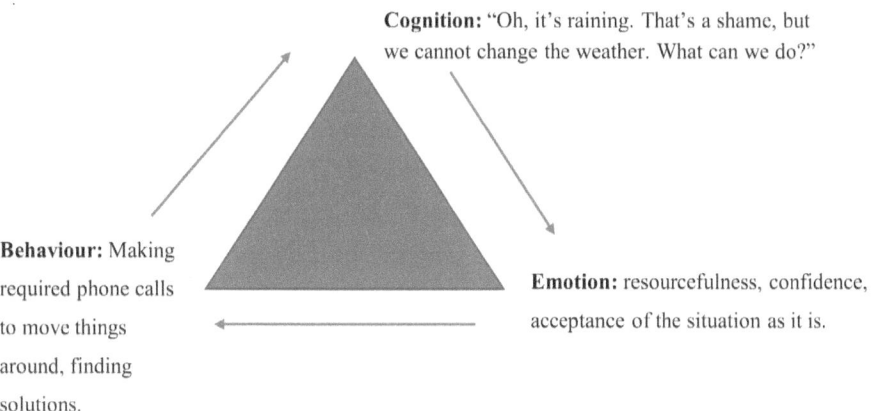

In the above diagram, the person decided to perceive the situation from a different perspective, which changed the entire cycle – creating a spiral of 'hope and determination'.

Although CBT has many decades behind it to back it up, it has also been criticised. One such critique is that CBT focused too heavily on challenging the person's thoughts and perceptions, which is hard work, and bypasses the emotional aspect of the situation.

Acceptance Commitment Therapy (ACT): This therapy has become more popular in the last decade and has positioned itself as the answer to CBT. The idea behind ACT is that as human beings, we will go through life experiencing a range of emotions as part of being human, such as joy, hatred, excitement, sadness, anticipation, resentment.

However, most people try to avoid strong negative feelings as much as possible, using any distraction available, including food, sex, gambling, alcohol or reality TV. The idea behind ACT is that trying to avoid emotions or resisting them creates even more psychological difficulties. People also tend to punish themselves for feeling a certain way, such as: *'I was feeling really sad yesterday, but then I thought how ungrateful I was feeling this way when other people have it worse. So, I felt guilty and ashamed for being sad.'*

Indeed, I had a client who came to therapy with this exact issue. This client was sensitive to the many negative things that were happening in the world and they could not shake off the feeling of guilt because their own life was going comparatively well. During the session, they also expressed feeling ashamed about coming to see a psychologist when there are people out there who are hungry or living in a war-torn nation. Unfortunately, their guilt about seeing a psychologist *'when other people have it worse'* was so strong that they only attended one session.

A word on emotions

Something that I often talk to my clients about is that we are able to experience **multiple, seemingly contradictory, emotions simultaneously**. One can feel empathy for someone else's misfortune *while at the same time* feeling grateful for what they have. One can acknowledge war, destruction, injustice in the world and *at the same time* acknowledge that they still need their own needs met and they deserve support and validation of their conflicting emotions. We can have all these emotions co-existing within us and they are all valid.

In our day-to-day life this is potentially easy to miss but pay attention next time you watch a movie, which often feature polarised characters:

the villain and the hero within an emotionally-charged story. You might catch yourself feeling angry with the villain while simultaneously feeling sorry for the hero, or if there is a plot twist and the villain shows vulnerability, you may feel empathy or mixed feelings for them.

Emotions are there to be felt. Their purpose is to indicate to us that something is happening: e.g., if we are feeling angry – this can indicate that an injustice had occurred, or we are in a position where we must defend ourselves; if we are feeling overwhelmed – too much is going on at once. Emotions just want our attention. As soon as we acknowledge that they are here, they reduce in intensity or go away.

Sitting with emotions

ACT and Emotion-Focused Therapy (EFT) share similar exercises that invite the client to go within and spend time allowing their emotions to be present without pushing them away, judging them or distracting themselves with something else. My clients often don't believe me, but the exercise of sitting with their emotions and acknowledging them takes around 10 minutes. The exercises can be slightly different. As an example, during an exercise, the person takes a few deep breaths and imagines as if they were a curious scientist who was trying to understand their emotions better. The therapist guides the person with questions such as: *'Where do you feel this sensation in or around your body? Does it have a particular shape? Is there a colour to it? Is it feeling hot, cold, or room temperature?'*. During the entire exercise, there are no attempts to get rid of the sensation. On the contrary, the focus is to understand it better without judging it, and to allow it to be there. The exercise can get deeper to understand the feeling even more and by the end of it for most people the sensation either significantly eases or dissipates. It wanted the person's attention and the exercises gave the opportunity to give it attention in a calm and non-judgemental way.

What's Normal Anyway

There are a lot of exercises involved in ACT, all focusing on acceptance, rather than forcing or pushing something. Many of the exercises are quite different to what one would normally expect in a counselling session, but they are effective, have been researched and many of them are a lot of fun, both for the client and for the practitioner. In Melbourne, we are lucky to have Dr Russ Harris, an internationally acclaimed ACT trainer. I have had the pleasure of attending quite a few workshops by Mr. Harris and would encourage you to do the same if you can, as he is a very engaging speaker. He has a lot of free resources that I'll add at the end of this chapter.

How do I know what therapy is right for me/my issue?

1. Consider your personality:
   - If you are a 'go-getter' with no time to waste and a desire to resolve a specific issue, start by looking up a professional with knowledge of short-term therapies, like SFBT and ACT.
   - If you are happy to invest more time to really understand what is happening within you, then a longer-term type of therapy, like Internal Family Systems, EFT, Schema, Gestalt and Psychotherapy could work best for you.
   - If you're a creative person, then perhaps finding a therapist who works through Art Therapy, Play-Based Therapy or Narrative Therapy would be a good starting point.

2. Consider the issue you need assistance with:
   - If your concern is trauma, then therapies which were created with a focus on trauma would be a good start: EFT, EMDR and the CBT subtype of therapy for trauma, such as Prolonged Exposure Therapy.

- For anxiety and depression, CBT and ACT work well, but in different ways.
- For addictive behaviour, Motivational Interviewing is the go-to therapy, as well as combinations from CBT, ACT and SFBT.
- For family concerns, a family therapist would be a starting point.
- For relationship concerns, a couple's therapist would be the most appropriate option.

3. Consider your preferred learning style: what is the easiest way for you to learn new information? Is it through seeing images and diagrams, listening to guided tapes/podcasts/audio files? Is it through experiential learning, by trying something and seeing what works? This information will be helpful when you see the therapist, so they can match the techniques to your preferred learning style.

SUMMARY

In this chapter, I outlined the most popular psychological therapies that are currently used by mental health professionals. I covered the differences between these therapies and when it is appropriate to use them. I also outlined pointers for you to decide what therapy could be your starting point, depending on your concerns, personality and preferred learning style.

Additional information

ACT – Acceptance-Commitment Therapy:
www.actmindfully.com.au – free resources and information on ACT.

EFT – Emotion-Focused Therapy: Australian Institute of Emotion-Focused Therapy: www.aieft.org.au.

EMDR – Eye Movement Desensitisation and Reprocessing:
- The EMDR International Association (www.emdria.org)
- EMDR Association of Australia lists accredited practitioners on: www.emdraa.org.

CBT – Cognitive Behavioural Therapy:
- Psychology tools, self-help tab, 'Thoughts in CBT': www.psychologytools.com/self-help/thoughts-in-cbt
- Moodgym – a free, interactive program that identifies whether you have symptoms of anxiety and depression that require further assistance and teaches skills to assist with the symptoms. www.moodgym.com.au
- CBT Australia – www.cbtaustralia.com.au

Chapter 7

The Power of Your Intuition

'You could have an intellectual ability, but if you can sharpen your intuition, which they say is emotion and intellect joining together, then a knowingness occurs.'
— **David Lynch**

In the previous chapters, we looked at how to choose the right professional for you in terms of their qualifications, therapeutic approach, as well as factors that are important to you, such as the person's gender, age and cultural orientation. This preparation is important to maximise the chances of developing a good professional partnership. In this chapter, we will delve even deeper on how to know whether the person you have chosen is indeed the right fit for you.

What's Normal Anyway

The importance of finding a good fit

Research over the past 50 years has consistently demonstrated that the therapeutic relationship, also referred to as the 'therapeutic alliance', is one of the most important factors that determines success in therapy.

According to a widely cited article by Michael J. Lambert (1989), this is the percentage breakdown of the different factors that play a part in the success of therapy:

- The technique that the therapist uses, their skills and knowledge – 15 per cent
- The relationship between the client and the therapist – 30 per cent
- The client's level of hope that therapy is going to work – 15 per cent
- The client's skills, resources, social supports – 40 per cent

Thus, 30 per cent of success in therapy is attributed to the quality of the professional relationship between the therapist and the client. According to the literature on this topic, the important components of a good therapeutic alliance include:

- The therapist and client agreeing together on therapy goals and working collaboratively
- The therapist demonstrating empathy, openness and a genuine desire to assist the client
- A recognition that ultimately the client is the expert on their difficulties
- The therapist seeking the client's feedback on the therapy process and making adjustments based on that feedback
- The client and the therapist repairing the relationship if/when misunderstandings occur

Open and honest communication between clients and therapists is very important in order to minimise and/or quickly resolve misunderstandings. We are all human, and at times we may not fully understand what the other person is trying to say. In Edward Teyber's brilliant book, *Interpersonal Process in Therapy: An Integrative Model* (2006), he **normalised** misunderstandings or challenges that can at times occur in a therapeutic relationship, stating that they are to be expected, just as misunderstandings and challenges occur in other significant relationships. Thus, misunderstandings between clients and therapists can occur at times and will require the courage to speak up, ask for clarification or express that something does not feel right. Indeed, the therapeutic process is a two-way street and a team effort between the therapist and the client.

In my experience, I have found that building trust between myself and the client is definitely the cornerstone of our work together. Often, people who come to see me have had previous experiences of being let down, hurt and at times even rejected by those closest to them. The mere act of seeing a stranger is already an act of bravery, let alone opening up to that person, which can at times take many weeks, months, or even years. I have certainly found that patience is important here; allowing time for both parties to get to know each other and build trust, which in most cases is the cornerstone of the therapeutic process.

Finding a psychologist is like finding a professional best friend

A psychologist (or another mental health professional of your choice) is a person to whom you will be disclosing *a lot* of personal information. This is potentially information that you have never disclosed to anyone else before. Although they are a professional, you still want to make sure that you open up to someone you can trust.

It's a delicate balance between giving the person all relevant information to assess whether they can help you, to diving in too deeply, too quickly with your story. The deeper you go into telling your story, the more disheartening it can be to realise that the person is not a good fit for you and that you need to find someone else and start again. In the first few sessions, both you and therapist are assessing each other. They are assessing whether they are able to assist you and you might also be assessing whether you'd like to continue working with them. This is an important part to focus on, as it is in these early moments that you can start getting cues whether this professional relationship is a good fit for you.

How long it will take to trust a complete stranger with your life story depends on your past life experiences and other factors. There is no rush. You have potentially carried your difficulties for decades. It is okay to take your time, especially if you have a history of trauma, so please do take the time you feel you need with this process.

Anxiety is actually your friend

Expect that you are likely to feel nervous in the lead-up to meeting the therapist. First and foremost, your brain is designed to keep you safe, and in order to keep you safe, it constantly scans for potential danger. The danger can be physical, as well as emotional, financial or social. The brain does not care exactly what is out there, it just wants you to be safe. Meeting a professional puts you in a vulnerable position. As we discussed in previous chapters, no matter how lovely, genuine and helpful the person is, they are in a position of power.

The Power of Your Intuition

Thus, your brain will naturally see this as a potentially dangerous situation, so be prepared to feel butterflies in your stomach, maybe some sweating, perhaps worrying thoughts about how the meeting will go or preparing for the worst-case scenario so you're not disappointed if it does not work out. There is also a chance that you will be tempted to cancel or postpone the meeting. This is your brain doing *exactly* what it was designed to do: keeping you in your comfort zone, away from anything or anyone who might hurt you. It is all to be expected. You can even say to your brain: *'Thanks, brain. I appreciate you looking out for me.'*

As tempting as it may be, *please do keep your first session*. You can bring another person along if it makes you feel comfortable or tell someone you trust that you have the meeting scheduled so that they can support you if you are starting to have doubts about attending the session.

Can I tell you a secret?

The person who you'll be meeting is human too. Even though they are a professional, they too, are likely to feel at least a little bit nervous before meeting you. I always feel a little bit nervous before meeting a new client, wondering what they will be like and what concerns they will have. However, it is likely that you'll meet your professional on their 'turf' or 'territory', so their anxiety will be less than yours, but there will still be some anxiety and no amount of psychology studies will eradicate that. We are all human at the end of the day. Allow yourself to feel that nervousness, knowing that this is a typical reaction by your brain to a new and unfamiliar situation.

What's Normal Anyway

Important things to notice in the first session

1. **How you feel in this person's presence**

    We already established that you will be initially feel some nervousness. That is normal and to be expected. This could last for the first 10-15 minutes. However, check-in with yourself how you are feeling half-way, or around 45 minutes into the session? Is there tension, annoyance or confusion, or do you notice yourself feeling calmer as the session progresses? None of these emotions are right or wrong, and initially they may not indicate anything about whether the person is a good fit or not. However, checking-in with yourself is a good practise to get into to start noticing how you are feeling in the session. This gives you at least a 'base-line' to go from. For example, *'I felt very nervous when I came into the room, but I am walking out feeling more at ease.'*

2. **The person's communication style – verbal and non-verbal**

    Notice how the person conducts the session. Their style is not necessarily 'right' or 'wrong', the question is how you *feel* about it. The first session often involves the professional introducing themselves, explaining how the sessions will be conducted, asking you questions, perhaps administering a questionnaire to assess where you are at (if that is part of their process) and listening most of the time. By the second and third session it tends to become even clearer how they work.

    During the first session, start noticing things like: Were they asking questions to understand you and your situation better? Did you feel heard? Were they respectful of your personal beliefs, be they cultural, religious or other aspects? Did they

The Power of Your Intuition

push for information that you felt was too early to disclose in the first or second session? Use these questions to gauge their interest in understanding what brought you to therapy.

I usually recommend that people try out a psychologist/therapist for at least two sessions to suss out whether they are a good fit, as the psychologist/therapist may be nervous as well. However, racist or culturally or otherwise insensitive jokes and comments are never appropriate and especially in the first or second session, they are a major red flag.

When I was a new mum of a newborn, I went to see a psychologist who I had never seen before. Being very sleep-deprived, emotional and just exhausted, I did not research anything about the person before our session – I just wanted to see someone as soon as possible. The majority of the session was a blur, but towards the end of it, the psychologist, knowing that I am Jewish, stated something along the lines of: *'Jewish people don't have a sense of humour because of their difficult past.'* Not only is this statement completely false, but it is also highly inappropriate and irrelevant to the conversation. There is no context where such a comment would be appropriate to say to any client. I left the session feeling shocked and knew that had I been thinking more clearly, I either would've responded on the spot or given verbal feedback at the next session about how her comment made me feel. Or, if I had the mental and physical strength for it, I would have potentially lodged a complaint. However, I was already a sleep-deprived and emotionally fatigued new parent, so I simply did not return. When you see any professional and especially a mental health professional, you have the right to be treated with respect and sensitivity.

3. **Check-in with yourself after the session. How did you feel afterwards?**
   - Did you feel heard?
   - Did you feel that the professional understood your situation or at least made a noticeable effort to understand it?
   - Do they seem to have a good knowledge of the issue that you need assistance with?

It is okay if after the first session you're still unsure whether you wish to proceed to the next. I would encourage you to reflect on what was happening for you during and after the session and, as mentioned previously, I would give the person at least two sessions to make up your mind if they are a good match to assist you with what you're looking for.

Disclosures of trauma: a word of warning!

This section is specifically for people who have booked a session with a new therapist in relation to something 'minor', in order to see whether this therapist can be trusted with something deeper, such as childhood trauma.

It is perfectly fine to 'suss out' whether the person you are seeing can be trusted with heavier issues. However, there are a few things to keep in mind to ensure your psychological safety. If the therapist believes that you are coming to see them for work stress when in reality you are eager to process traumatic childhood experience/s, then I would encourage you to **let the therapist know earlier in the session** that you are hoping to discuss something of a traumatic nature. Whether you'll be able to disclose the information on the same day or not will depend on you, the therapist and how much time is available. However, what is important is for the therapist to have the 'heads up' that this is on your mind.

The Power of Your Intuition

I have had experiences where clients spent an entire session talking about their 'minor' concerns and then five minutes before the session was about to end, without any prior warning, they disclosed details of childhood trauma. Revealing something of this nature five minutes before the session is ending does not give the therapist and the client adequate time to process all the feelings that might come with that disclosure, and this **compromises the client's safety**.

Usually, at the end of the session, the therapist spends time to make sure that the client is emotionally and physically safe to leave and to continue with the rest of their day and week. If a significant revelation occurs at the end of the session, rushed decisions then need to be made to ensure that the client remains psychologically and physically safe as talking about traumatic experiences can cause distress.

Research also has shown that people with significant trauma, especially if they have never disclosed it to anyone before, might feel very eager to finally get it off their chest when they first see a therapist. However, once the disclosure occurs, some people can experience a great sense of shame at the realisation that they have now revealed a very personal story to a complete stranger. Thus, care needs to be taken with sensitive disclosures, both in terms of ensuring that the therapist is aware that you wish to bring them up and in making sure that you disclose it to a person you trust.

What if I don't like the therapist even after the second or third session, but I'm worried about hurting their feelings, so I keep attending the sessions?

You have the right to choose a professional in whom you have confidence. If you are not satisfied that they are the right fit for you, do not hang around for six or more sessions because you don't want to hurt their feelings. It is not about them, but rather what you are getting out of the sessions. The therapist will be okay. You need to do what is right for you.

If people-pleasing is the reason that you're coming to see a mental health professional in the first place and you are still feeling uncertainty and guilt about stopping the sessions, here are a few ways to handle the situation:

1. See this as an opportunity for you to practise your communication skills and boundary setting. Consider if you'd be willing to talk about this with your treating professional. Chapter 9 discusses techniques around communication in general and with your treating professional in more depth.
2. View the situation as a business transaction – because it is. You are paying for a service. If the service provider is not meeting your needs, it is okay to find another service provider. If you were going to a restaurant and they were selling food that you did not enjoy, you wouldn't keep going to the same restaurant, would you? **This is not personal**. Repeat this to yourself as many times as needed.
3. An ethical professional would not use their power to push, manipulate or guilt you into continuing sessions with them if you don't wish to, and they certainly would not take it personally if you don't wish to see them again.

How long is too long?

Most people would know by the third or fourth session whether the professional is right for them. However, be honest and examine within yourself whether there is a part of you that does not want to attend sessions not because of the person, but because *the topic of discussion is unpleasant or uncomfortable to discuss*. Edward Tayber (2006) addressed this in his book when he noted that there is often ambivalence about attending therapy: on the one hand, the person wants to feel better, but on the other hand, attending sessions involves touching on challenging topics. If this is your concern, I would encourage you to discuss it with your practitioner.

One of my clients was very open with me about feeling this way. Around session three, I asked her for feedback about how she felt during therapy and whether there were things that did not feel right to her. She replied, *'I have to force myself to come here. Don't get me wrong, I like coming in to see you, but I dread talking about my anxiety.'* I validated her feelings and we discussed what we could add to the process. In this client's case, I recommended particular books for her to read between the sessions, as they addressed anxiety-related concerns and she could go over the exercises in private. Our sessions were then used to help her clarify things and extend her home learning. I was able to come up with a solution only because we had the conversation, and she was able to honestly tell me how she felt about coming to our sessions.

What if I don't trust my own judgement or I'm too shy/scared to attend the first session alone?

This is more common than you may think. I often have people coming in for the first, or the first few sessions with a support person: a significant other, sibling, close friend or family member. I think that it is a good idea to bring someone with you if you're nervous. Perhaps let the therapist know in advance if you can, so that they can prepare an extra chair and ensure that there is enough space for everyone to feel comfortable.

It also gives you another pair of eyes and ears. You might feel too nervous to take in all the information or might forget significant facts that your loved could remind you of. It is often nice for the professional to meet people in your life who are important to you and they can receive additional information about you and what you are going through from the perspective of your loved one.

This chapter is titled *The Power of Your Intuition*. This is because discerning whether the professional who you are seeing is right for you requires you to tune into your feelings and trusting what you are feeling.

If you're interested, below are some suggested activities that you can play with to develop your self-trust. They are adapted from the book *Developing Intuition: Practical Guidance for Daily Life* (2000) by Shakti Gawain. The book includes additional exercises and can be found online or in your local library or bookstore.

It is not mandatory for you to trial these exercises, but I have added them in for a bit of fun if you would like to enhance your levels of self-trust.

Activities to enhance your self-trust

Recall situations or incidents when you had a strong gut feeling about something or someone and *you were right*:

Situation 1

_____
_____
_____
_____
_____

The Power of Your Intuition

_____
_____
_____

Situation 2

_____
_____
_____
_____
_____
_____
_____

Did you experience the feeling anywhere in your body?

_____
_____
_____
_____
_____
_____
_____

We all have an in-built 'truth' radar that tells us what is right for us, even if others disagree. To tune in to your gut feeling, start with asking yourself guided questions about seemingly insignificant things, like, *'Should I go first to the supermarket or to the greengrocer today?'* or

'How do I feel about speaking to so and so today?' and then notice how you are feeling. What is coming up for you? Be curious about the sensations. The purpose of the exercise is to connect to yourself and to tune in to your preferences.

SUMMARY

In this chapter, we covered what to look out for during the first few meetings with a new professional to increase the likelihood that you're investing your time and money in a person who is right for you. Working with a therapist is indeed an investment. It is worth going through the steps of discernment to find the right match for you, as your therapist could become a mentor and a source of professional support for many years to come.

Additional resources

Gawain, S. (2000). *Developing Intuition: Practical Guidance for Daily Life*. Nataraj Publishing.

References

Lambert, M.J. (1989). The individual therapist's contribution to psychotherapy process and outcome. *Clinical Psychology Review, 9* (4), 469-485.

Teyber, E. (2006). *Interpersonal Process in Therapy: An Integrative Model* (5th ed.). Thompson Brooks/Cole.

Chapter 8

The Power of Backing Yourself

Our previous chapters focused on increasing your chances of success in therapy by choosing a therapist who is most aligned with your values and goals. However, there is another factor that we need to address: your expectations of yourself and of how quickly you'll see results.

> 'Set realistic goals, keep re-evaluating and be consistent.'
> **– Venus Williams**

We will look at an example of weight loss to demonstrate this point. Many of us have been there. We have gained some weight and then we saw an exciting advertisement of a new, revolutionary 'magic bullet' that would help us shed a few kilograms or pounds in a record time! How exciting! Who doesn't like fast results? So, we purchased this new exercise program, or weight loss shakes, or whatever else was being marketed to us, and our energy and motivation were initially high: we exercised every day, followed the meal plan, took measurements…

Within two to three weeks, we have been able to reduce a centimetre here or there, maybe a few grams on the scale, but for the amount of work that we invested, it did not seem like the results matched our efforts. We probably felt deflated and potentially even gave up. Can you relate?

Well, in psychology, initially it can be even more difficult to spot your progress! There are no body measurements and nobody takes photos of you 'before therapy', 'during therapy' and 'after therapy'. Psychologists and other mental health professionals have created different scales and questionnaires that measure the symptoms of various psychological conditions. Many therapists use these to track their clients' progress, and we will go over the most common measurement tools in Chapter 10. However, not all therapists use measurement tools, and even if they do, not every issue that brings people to counselling can be measured.

Just like weight loss (or any other goal that you set for yourself), it is understandable that you would want to know that the effort of doing the work will actually pay off and there will be tangible results! It is the same with attending therapy.

Many people who attend therapy do so to achieve specific goals. For example, they want to see that their:

- Mood improves
- Relationships are more settled

The Power of Backing Yourself

- Anxiety and depression are alleviated
- Overall functioning is improved

And yet…

Because we want to get better, yet the process itself brings up uncomfortable feelings and requires us to make changes, you may have days where you will:

- Doubt whether you can actually change/get better
- Worry that you're wasting your/the therapist's time
- Wonder if you're ever going to see results
- Worry whether you can maintain the progress once therapy ends

Facing challenging topics can bring up resistance. More than once I have had clients who 'needed the toilet' right in the middle of a difficult discussion, changed topics to something unrelated to the discussion, ran late to the sessions or unexpectedly could not make it to sessions for various reasons. Of course, life and emergencies happen. It is when emergencies, sudden cancellation and/or late attendances become a **pattern** that most therapists start to wonder what is going on for the client. Not always, but sometimes, these could be indicators of resistance. *'Working with resistance is a normal part of treatment'* (Teyber, 2006, p.83).

> *'Any change, even a change for the better, is always accompanied by drawbacks and discomforts.'*
> **– Arnold Bennett**

As indicated above, resistance to change is normal, and I respect it when I see it happening in my clients. When I note their resistance, I bring it up for discussion so it is now out in the open and can be assessed and processed in the safety of the therapeutic partnership.

The good news

A lot of the material that people bring to therapy is **learned behaviour**. If a behaviour is learned, this means it can be **unlearned!** The not-so-good news is that learning something new requires practise and can take time. As with the weight loss example, it involves learning new ways of doing something and then putting it into practise, getting it wrong, having a day when things don't go to plan, then trying again.

Weight often takes many months or years to put it on, so it is likely to take more than two to three weeks of exercise and healthy eating to start seeing substantial results. With psychology as well, there are some thinking and behavioural habits that we have formed and potentially practised *for many decades, over and over again*. Depending on the situation, it can take more than a few sessions to start to turn things around.

Tips for starting anything new and unfamiliar, including therapy

- Congratulate yourself for starting! Putting yourself in a situation where you are handing over some control to someone else in order to improve your life and relationships is a big deal. Changing yourself is the hardest thing to do. Even by picking up this book, you have opened up your mind to the possibility that you can learn something new. We *all* can

always learn something new. I take my hat off to you for being willing to learn new things!
- Give yourself grace and compassion, especially when you're feeling stuck, or feeling that no progress is being made. Similar to a weight loss journey, seeing tangible results can take time and it is even more challenging to notice the subtle changes in your communications skills, decision-making, boundary-setting and handling previously daunting situations with greater ease.
- Expect to experience resistance to attending therapy, as well as having doubts about whether you actually need to attend or whether it will make any difference at all. This is all normal so bring it up with your therapist. Therapists know that it takes a lot of courage and/or pain to commit to counselling sessions and will talk through any doubts with you.
- Remind yourself that you are running your own race. This is not a competition where the first client to reach their goals wins a prize. This is you taking charge of your life and making a commitment to yourself to get out of your comfort zone with the support and assistance of your professional, or your team of health professionals.

Hot tip

Please resist the temptation to compare yourself to other imaginary clients that your professional is potentially seeing. One of my pet peeves is when a client asks, *'Am I the worst case that you've ever seen?'* Perhaps some health professionals are able to answer this question. However, I cannot, and when a client asks this, I see it as a waste of our focus and energy. Imagine if I was actually sitting around and ranking my clients: *'Let me open my Excel spreadsheet of my worst cases, Debbie and I'll tell you exactly where you are ranked today. Ooh, sorry,*

What's Normal Anyway

Debbie, it looks like Brian overtook you last week with his story, so he is the worst case that I've ever seen. However, you don't know how next week will be for you, anything can happen!'

You're an individual. Debbie is an individual. Brian is an individual. Their stories are as unique as they are and there really is no competition about 'who is worse'. Your journey is your own. Put your energy and focus into getting closer to **your** specific goals and don't worry about how anyone else compares, as everyone is running their own sprint or marathon.

When is it realistic to start seeing results in therapy?

This is a fair question, and the answer depends on the issue that brought you to therapy, your goals and your history.

In previous chapters, I introduced Michael Lambert's breakdown of the different factors that contribute to success in therapy. According to his research, around **55 per cent of success in therapy is due to client-related factors,** such the client's level of hope that the therapy would work, the skills and resources that they bring to therapy, as well as their environment (how much social support they have, the environment that they live in, etc).

This is the breakdown of percentages once more:

- The client's level of hope that therapy is going to work – 15 per cent
- The quality of the client's participation in treatment, their skills and resources, social supports and the environment in which they live – 40 per cent
- The therapist's technique, skills and knowledge – 15 per cent
- The relationship between the client and therapist – 30 per cent

As you can see from this breakdown, the client is the most important factor in therapy and everything happens with their participation. I have had clients who achieved their therapy goal in the first session and attended the second session only to 'tie up loose ends'. For the most part, these were clients who:

- Had no previous concerns regarding their psychological health
- Faced a single unexpected incident that triggered a strong response within them that was appropriate to the situation
- Had good support around them and had helpful coping strategies before the incident

On the other end of the spectrum, there are clients I have regularly seen for a few years. These are clients who often have:

- Chronic physiological conditions that impact on their psychological health
- Learning disabilities or an intellectual disability
- A complex childhood background
- Limited social support around them

In this case, it is unrealistic to expect immediate results and the progress is often slower. Most people will be somewhere in between. With some people four to six sessions will be enough to reach particular goals, while in other cases, 10 or more sessions will be required.

Trial and error

When you're starting to work with a new therapist, it is all trial and error. You and the therapist don't know each other well yet, and whilst on paper a lot of techniques and strategies could work, it is a process of discovery. A few things may be new for you, some strategies could seem really 'weird' and other strategies you may have tried in the past with little success and therefore have little hope that they'll work for you in future (like meditation, that many people may struggle with initially), but what if these things *could* work in this new professional relationship?

I would encourage you to keep an open mind, while still constantly checking in with yourself about how you feel about the therapist and the atmosphere in the sessions, as discussed in the last chapter.

Everything starts and ends with your feedback

We covered at the start of the book that your psychologist cannot read your mind. This means that they are relying on *your feedback* to correct the course of treatment. Especially when you're going home with a new set of exercises to trial, notice how you feel doing them and come back with feedback for the next session.

What if my feedback offends the psychologist?

It won't if they are a true professional. The sessions are not about your psychologist, they are about you and what **you** want to get out of the sessions. Remember that you and the psychologist are on the same team and it is their desire for you to succeed. They studied for years to get the opportunity to help others. You have already made the most difficult step by coming into therapy, so you might as well make the most of it.

This is also a good time to start practicing communicating with your therapist as honestly as possible, thus deepening the relationship and working on your communication skills, which we will cover in the next chapter.

The Power of Backing Yourself

What if, despite my efforts, I am still not progressing?

This is something to bring up with your therapist. Perhaps there are things in your environment that are impacting your progress, or maybe self-doubt and thoughts of quitting therapy too early are starting to creep in?

There is also the possibility that, in addition to therapy, other treatments perhaps can be considered, such as medications or support groups. In Australia, if a client is referred under Medicare, then after the sixth session a progress report needs to be sent to their GP. I use this marker to evaluate the effectiveness of the treatment up to this point. I expect that by the sixth session, there will be some changes in how the person is feeling. However, if there is no progress, this is my cue to discuss additional options.

EXERCISES FOR REFLECTION

1. Reflect and note below whether there are areas in your life where you place unrealistic expectations on yourself? This could be in relation to the state of cleanliness of your home, how healthy your meals should be, how much time you should be spending with your children or other loved ones, or how productive you should be at work – no matter what is going on or how you are feeling.

The Power of Backing Yourself

2. Identify ambivalence/resistance to attending therapy. Complete the following sentence: *'Of course I want to feel better, but...'* For example, *'Of course I want to feel better, but the therapy may involve too much effort'* or, *'Of course I want to feel better, but I don't think that I can reveal my true thoughts to the therapist – I feel too embarrassed.'* Use the space below and keep repeating this sentence to uncover additional resistance points.

It is valuable to become aware of these concerns so you can examine them further. Perhaps, if you're comfortable, you could bring them up with your therapist. Many of your concerns will be valid. This is how your brain tries to keep you safe, so please refrain from self-judgement and focus on the changes that you would like to achieve.

3. Project into the future: If nothing changes right now, how will your life look in a year? How will it look like in three years? Look at areas such as family relationships, work, recreational activities, physical health and other areas that are important to you.

_____
_____
_____
_____
_____
_____

4. Allow yourself to dream. Complete this sentence: *'What if my therapy **is** a success? What **would** be different in my life?'*

_____
_____
_____
_____
_____
_____

References

Lambert, M.J. (1989). The individual therapist's contribution to psychotherapy process and outcome. *Clinical Psychology Review, 9* (4), 469-485.

Teyber, E. (2006). *Interpersonal Process in Therapy: An Integrative Model* (5th ed.). Thompson Brooks/Cole.

Chapter 9

The Power of Courageous Communication

'Words are singularly the most powerful force available to humanity. We can choose to use this force constructively with words of encouragement, or destructively using words of despair. Words have energy and power with the ability to help, to heal, to hinder, to hurt, to harm, to humiliate and to humble.'
— **Yehuda Berg**

This is the longest chapter in the book, and I consider it one of the core chapters. Now that we have established how to find the practitioner who is right for you, let's go through one of the main concerns that brings people to my office: interpersonal communication.

Specifically, this chapter will unpack:

- What helps and hinders effective communication
- Four styles of communication
- A communication formula to get your thoughts across in a peaceful and organised manner that will increase your chances of getting your needs met
- Surprising ways in which your therapy sessions can help build your communication skills

Why is this important?

Many of us have not had great role models when it came to communication. Communication was not something that was formally taught and yet we were expected to *'show respect'* and *'use your words'* to verbally express needs and wants from a young age. Similar to emotions, it was expected that kids would just *know* how to communicate effectively. The problem is that no one taught our parents either.

Most of us were trained to be obedient growing up, as well as to:

- Not cause a scene
- Not rock the boat
- Be polite, especially towards those in a position of authority (parents, teachers, bosses)
- Be seen and not heard
- Get over grievances quickly and forget about them
- Not hold a grudge, especially towards adults or those in a position of authority
- Speak only when spoken to
- Not say anything that might upset anyone else

The Power of Courageous Communication

Many of us grew up with the message: *'Put other people's needs ahead of yours. You'll be fine. Just get through this.'* I know that, as a female, I was definitely socialised to be quiet, neat, modest, polite and certainly not to talk back to the adults.

The problem with this type of socialisation is that, just like with buried emotions, what we don't express stays buried inside and comes out in other ways. Over time, hurt, resentment, unmet needs and unspoken words can express themselves as:

- Physical or emotional illness
- Perpetual sadness or aggression due to inability to express what weighs on us
- Addictions or other self-harming behaviour
- Misunderstandings and conflict in close relationships
- Conflict avoidance at all costs
- People-pleasing at the expense of our own wants and needs

Although communication patterns are not genetic, they are passed down from one generation to the next as *learned behaviour.* If you reflect on your own upbringing, you may notice that the way your parents communicated (or did not communicate) with you was potentially how your grandparents communicated (or did not communicate) with your parents. If you have your own children, the pattern becomes even more obvious as you are potentially repeating to your children the same phrases that you heard while growing up.

Reflecting on this might bring up painful memories, especially if caregivers or other adults in a position of authority used offensive language, name-calling and used verbal or physical punishment for expressing thoughts and feelings. The good news, however, is that bringing this to our attention means that we can do something about it. Since communication is *learned behaviour,* then we can *learn* better ways to communicate! This will not erase the past, but it can improve aspects of our relationships in the present and in the future.

'Awareness is the first step in healing.'
— **Dean Ornish**

Did you know?

From a biological perspective, it makes perfect sense that communication is not our strongest point as a species. If we go back to the times of the cavemen, they had only the basic survival instincts: breathing, hunger, thirst, the sleep cycle, procreation, self-preservation and strong emotions such as fear, anger and anxiety. All of the instincts that we require for our survival are located in the same part of the brain, tucked away deeply within it (as it is so vital for our survival) and connected to our spinal cord. This part of the brain is called the limbic system.

The important thing to remember with the limbic system is that it is responsible for body functions that happen *automatically*. That is, they happen without our conscious control. You don't usually sit and consciously decide if you will inhale or exhale. The body does it for you without you having to think about it. The modern human has evolved and adapted since the days of the cavemen and has parts of the brain that the cavemen did not have. Specifically, the modern man has *the frontal lobe*, which is the area of your forehead. The frontal lobe is important for functions such as: planning ahead, decision-making, gathering information, remembering previous experiences, morals and ethics, empathy, speech and language production, understanding other people's emotions, motivation, managing attention and forming personality (Villines, 2017).

The Power of Courageous Communication

If you're struggling with any of the above areas, take heart that from an evolutionary perspective we have not had this part of the brain with us for very long, so we are still practising and learning how to use its functions. As I've also mentioned in Chapter 3, the frontal lobe does not fully develop until a human is about 25 years of age.

To summarise this important section: our brains are designed to keep us **physically safe**, first and foremost. Communication using words was not a necessity for our survival as a species, so it was not a priority to develop this ability. Nowadays, the modern man has a frontal lobe which allows for more sophisticated communication. However, this part of the brain is relatively new for humans and requires conscious effort.

Moreover, from a biological perspective, all the basic functions that are needed for our survival will always take precedence. The 'higher' functions of our brain are activated once our basic needs have been met. This is an important point to remember for what we'll discuss in the rest of this chapter. If you can imagine seeing someone running out of the woods – hungry, thirsty, sleep-deprived, having just escaped a chase by a predator. The last thing on their mind will be to carefully choose their words using sophisticated language.

Easier to access once top priorities are satisfied: reasoning, communication, decision-making, empathy.

Top priority: survival.
Food, water, safety, shelter.

What's Normal Anyway

What does this mean for our communication?

As demonstrated by the example above, the structure of our brain means that we can struggle with taking in information, making a decision, empathising with another person or communicating effectively when we are:

- Hungry
- Tired
- Preoccupied with something else
- Intimidated – physically or verbally
- Scared for a loved one's safety
- In a hurry or feeling hurried

Additionally, concentrating on effective communication will be challenging if we are:

- Worried about the consequences of communication. If we are punished for our communication, then our brain will perceive communicating as a potential threat to our physical or mental health.
- Under the effects of drugs and alcohol, which affect the brain and impact on our perception, recognition of emotions and other aspects that are important in interpersonal communication (Harmsworth & Paulmann, 2018; NIDA, 2022).

Your brain will always prioritise your physical safety above anything else. If you are in a situation where the above conditions dominate, you must ensure that your physical needs are met first.

The above information is also important to remember when you are communicating with another person. If that person is feeling intimidated, cornered or verbally attacked by you, they will not be able to take in anything that you are saying. Their body will automatically go into survival mode and even if they do as you say, they will do so only out of fear and a desire to save themselves from your wrath.

In this next section, we will look at styles of communication, describe the benefits of assertive communication and introduce a **communication formula** to make challenging or anxiety-provoking conversations more manageable.

If you are looking to communicate with someone who is affected by drugs or alcohol, or if you wish to communicate with someone about their use of drugs and alcohol, you will find helpful tips on the Alcohol and Drug Foundation website: https://adf.org.au/talking-about-drugs/having-conversation/

Four styles of communication

In this section we will outline the four broad styles of communication. I am listing them here for the purpose of raising your awareness of your current communication style. At different points in your life, you will have potentially used each of these four styles to various degrees. If you recognise yourself in any of these styles, I hope that you will show yourself understanding and compassion and congratulate yourself on being willing to increase your awareness.

Below is not a dictionary definition of the styles, but rather my definitions based on my understanding of each of them:

- **Aggressive communication:** This style expresses itself as a heightened tone of voice, shouting, yelling, blaming, giving commands/orders that cannot be questioned, being highly critical, using belittling language and may include threats of physical harm, social humiliation, threats of legal action and blackmailing. In the era of online communication, aggressive communication can also happen via texts, emails, social media forums and can come from both strangers and people we know. Often, this communication style is seen in bullies and people who are eager to control others. It tends to stem from a place of insecurity and a fear that their insecurities will be exposed, as well as a strong need to 'win' at any cost.

- **Passive communication:** This is a style where individuals have learned to focus on meeting the needs and wishes of others at their own expense. Often these individuals have difficulty saying *'no'* and sometimes go along with unreasonable requests or orders that contradict their own needs and wishes. Individuals who use passive communication were either socialised from a young age to ignore what they wanted in order to appease others or learned to become passive as a result of frightening experiences that involved physical, emotional, social or financial repercussions for standing up for themselves. At times, it occurs out of a desire 'to fit in' and a fear of losing social connectedness.
- **Passive-aggressive communication:** This is often the result of prolonged passivity in the face of aggressors. The internal anger builds up, but if the person is not in a position to directly stand up to the aggressor, they show their displeasure through indirect ways that will not cause them harm, such as: anonymous revenge tactics, gossiping about the person, using sarcastic humour or pretending to like someone while sabotaging them.
- **Assertive communication:** This is the style of communication where you strike a balance between confidently saying what you mean, saying 'no' when you want to say 'no' without worrying that you will offend someone and, most importantly, where you recognise that your wants and needs matter too.

The Power of Courageous Communication

Bear in mind that people can use a mix of communication styles depending on the situation and who they are dealing with. Someone can be very assertive with their best friend but lean towards passive-aggressive communication in the company of a rude relative. This same individual may also behave in a very passive manner at work with their demanding boss, but use aggressive communication on their drive home in peak hour traffic. Thus, the same person can use all four styles of communication on the same day. Often, when people see a therapist in relation to their communication style, their aim is to increase the level of assertive communication in their lives.

Assertive communication style – a worthwhile goal

> *'Communication is a skill that you can learn. If you're willing to work at it, you can rapidly improve the quality of your life.'*
> **– Brian Tracy**

Indeed, assertive communication is a learned skill, and this is great news! It means that it can be developed and improved with practise.

Benefits of learning assertive communication:

1. When you are able to express yourself clearly, it makes it easier for the other person to deliver to you what you want. If your favourite restaurant is a Mexican restaurant down the road, but when your spouse asks you where you would like to go out for dinner, you say, *'Wherever you'd like'* or *'I don't mind,'* what is the likelihood that you'll go to your favourite restaurant? Not likely.
2. Learning how to communicate clearly and confidently allows you to maintain your boundaries. Boundaries are incredibly

important. They let other people know where you stand, and they protect your time and energy. Other people cannot read your mind and 'hints' rarely work. Learning assertive communication gives you the tools to clearly indicate what is or isn't acceptable to you.
3. You will increase your own levels of self-respect and self-value. Even if you were socialised to put others first, the only person who will always be with you is *you*. You might as well start investing in this relationship and ensuring that your needs and wants are also met.

It is hard to undo many decades of social conditioning, such as being 'the good girl', who went along with what others wanted for her; or the social conditioning of the man who makes all the decisions for his family, because he learned while growing up that this is a man's responsibility.

I often have men coming to my office who are so frustrated about their communication with their wives. Frequently, their wife grew up in an environment where she was taught to be quiet, not to ask for anything, not to demand too much, not to cause any friction and to be passive. In a marriage perhaps this worked for a certain period, but my male clients often attend the sessions and express frustration: *'I am sick of making every single decision. Where to go for a holiday, where to go on a weekend. Why can't my wife just tell me her preferences?'*

The women I speak to tell me that they find it difficult to directly express their preferences. They fear that they will be rejected by their friends or partners, or even fear that they will be abandoned and that no one will love them unless they go along with other people's wishes.

Challenges in communication, of course, also occur between friends, colleagues, parents and children (even adult children). We all could

The Power of Courageous Communication

benefit from communicating more clearly. Outline in the space below additional reasons that you can think of why it could be worthwhile for you to improve your own communication skills. What positive difference would it make in your life at work, with family members, with friends or with your life partner?

Anxiety about becoming an assertive communicator

Changing anything about your habits can be anxiety-provoking. You could be wondering if you have the strength and the resolve to do this and you could be wondering about the reaction of the people close to you if you start to change. These are valid concerns.

Please remember that you do not need to do anything drastic. In actual fact, it is better to start by making small, barely noticeable changes in your life while you are gaining confidence and finding what works. **Gradual change is what sticks.** The strategies below could provide a starting point. If you are seeing a psychologist, or another mental health professional, working with them on your specific situation will help you learn strategies that are tailored for you.

Practising assertiveness skills in counselling

One of my favourite exercises during a session is to help my clients practise their assertiveness skills and see them grow in confidence. You will be surprised how many people face regular bullying at work from colleagues or bosses, in their personal lives from 'friends' who take advantage of their kind nature and even from complete strangers in various settings.

Practising assertiveness is also useful in intimate relationships. For example, one of my clients wanted to become more assertive in order to improve communication with his wife. The client felt that he was being overly passive in his communication and was not sure how to change that. On one occasion, he described that he hoped to get a tattoo that was meaningful for him, but which his wife strongly objected to. My client booked an appointment to get the tattoo but was scared to let his wife know out of fear

The Power of Courageous Communication

that the discussion would escalate into an argument. He hoped to learn a calm and respectful way to talk about a topic that they had opposing views on.

In my session with my client, I introduced him to the same communication formula that I will shortly introduce to you, and then we had a few rounds of him practising the formula using a technique called **communication role-play.** Through this technique, he and I alternated being in the role of either the client or the wife. I wanted my client to experience the anxiety which comes with trying something very different and to see that, with repeat practise, his anxiety reduced and his confidence increased.

During the role-play, I could also monitor my client's tone of voice, body posture and his use of words. I noticed that my client was constantly apologising to his pretend 'wife', justifying himself and overall acting as if he had done something wrong. We practised having a steady tone of voice, listening to and validating his wife's concerns (she did have valid concerns) whilst at the same time being confident in the decision that he had made. We agreed that my client's wife has the right to her opinion, and he has the right to make a decision in relation to his own body. The purpose of the conversation was not to change her mind, but rather to convey his decision in a calm manner – not aggressively or apologetically either.

In the following session, my client came back to report that the conversation went better than he expected. Although his wife was still against the tattoo, he felt more empowered and was not trying to appease her. Instead, they agreed to disagree in a respectful and calm manner.

Please remember: if you are in a situation where your physical, emotional or social safety will be at risk if you speak up for yourself, the appropriate step is to contact an organisation that will assist you in taking steps to get safe. At the end of this chapter, I have listed details of such organisations.

Should you wish to try communicating more assertively, I will warn you right now: you *will* feel anxiety as you start practising. This is to be expected. Trying anything new brings with it feelings of uncertainty and apprehension. Of course, you can decide to continue doing what you have done so far. And what would happen then? The same people who text you only when they need your help but are never there for you will keep texting you when they need your help. The same people who ignore you when you need assistance, support or company will continue to ignore you. Why would they change the way they treat you, if you have not changed your stance on how you want to be treated?

> *'Sometimes if you want to see a change for the better, you have to take things into your own hands.'*
> **– Clint Eastwood**

How do I become more assertive?

There are a range of different communication strategies that you could try.

I am sharing a **communication formula** that I taught my client in the previous example, along with many other clients. This communication formula works really well for:

- Organising your thoughts and feelings before speaking.
- Deciding on the purpose of your communication: what exactly do you want to get out of this communication?
- Expressing your feelings without blaming the other person.

The Power of Courageous Communication

The formula is four sentences that you would need to complete:

> 1. I feel/felt…
> 2. When…
> 3. Because…
> 4. Instead, I would prefer it if…

Practising your formula

1. Please note that this formula is not something that we do naturally. As such, it will require some pre-thought and practise when you are alone, calm and clear-headed.
2. **You need to start by completing the last sentence first.** What is the outcome that you want? What do you ideally want to see/do? For example, if your partner always insists on going camping with a group of friends, but you would prefer to go camping with just him, or just him and your kids, then this would be your last sentence: *'I would prefer it if this year we went camping just you and I/ you, me and the kids.'*
3. Please pick only **ONE** specific event/problematic behaviour at a time. This is not an opportunity to bring up everything from the last decade. It will not work if you start with: *'Eight years ago, you ignored me at Betty's birthday party, then five years ago you did not comment on the new dress that I bought, and then three years ago I spent the evening alone while you worked.'* Bringing up multiple events from the past results in the message getting lost. The person will most likely feel attacked, won't know which event or accusation to address first and an argument is likely to start without anything being resolved.

4. Refrain from using words such as *'never'* and *'always'*. The use of these extreme words in a conversation will hurt others and will detract from the message. Look again at point two: what is the desired outcome: to argue or to reach a solution? When you communicate, try to use 'I' statements as much as possible: *'I feel, I noticed, I wonder'*. This makes it more difficult for the other person to argue with you. If you feel neglected, then that is how you feel. If you noticed a specific behaviour, then that is what you noticed.
5. I encourage you to start practising this formula on things/matters that are not significant. Small, gradual steps will bring about more effective results in the long run than trying to conquer Mount Everest in one day.
6. As you are practising, you will notice that some words need to be changed to make it flow better, but the idea should remain the same. Start practising it with insignificant matters to see how it works for you. This is also to make it fit your style and to build your confidence.

ADDITIONAL TIPS

When you feel ready to use the communication formula, ensure that the person receiving it is fed, calm and well rested.

Ask them if they have time to talk right now and if not, when will be a good time for them? This shows courtesy and respect and you're more likely to get them at a headspace when they are open for the conversation. They may prefer to talk when the kids have gone to bed or when their favourite TV show has finished.

The Power of Courageous Communication

Examples

Let's take an example of a grumpy teenager who gets snappy when we ask them: *'How was school today?'* Coming back to what we learned, we won't waste our time by asking the grumpy teenager anything. We will wait until the teenager had something to eat, had some rest and then when they felt calmer, we will first ask when would be a good time to talk.

Using the formula above, we could then state something along the lines of:

*'**I felt** worried **when** I noticed today that you were snappy after school **because** usually you are calm when you come home. **I would like** to understand what is happening for you.'*

I slightly changed the last sentence to make it flow better.

Another example could be in relation to something that you would like to watch on TV:

*'**I feel** irritated **when** I watch the news **because** they keep repeating the same negative information. **Instead, I would prefer it if** we could watch a comedy on Netflix.'*

A further example of practising this formula would be on something simple that you would like an answer to, such as: *'Honey, I was a bit **confused when** you bought rye bread from the store instead of sourdough **because** I was really hoping to have sourdough this week. I'm curious as to what happened there?'*

In this example, I have varied the formula to make it less formal and more conversational. You will have your own style of saying the same information but try to stick to the general rules.

As with everything, the more you practise the formula, the easier it will become. This is why I recommend starting with something that is low-risk and not truly important as a confidence-building exercise.

Practise your communication with your psychologist

If you already have a psychologist, I encourage you to practise your communication with them. Therapy is a mirror of what is happening in your daily life. The same communication style that you use in your daily life will eventually come into the sessions. This is fantastic for increasing your awareness.

There could be numerous ways that your communication style would manifest in the sessions. For example:

- If you are a people-pleaser and try to avoid conflict, you might tell your therapist that you're doing better than you actually are so that the therapist is pleased with you.
- If you use sarcasm with your friends or seek reassurance from others, then during therapy you will likely also be using sarcasm and seeking reassurance from your therapist.
- If outside the therapy room you cut people off when they are talking, then during sessions you might be doing exactly the same with your therapist.

Therapy is the perfect place to practise your communication skills with someone who is in your corner.

Additionally, in therapy, at times there will be miscommunication. It does not have to happen, but in every close relationship from time to time there can be misunderstandings. Ocassionaly in my work with my clients, I have said something that has confused them, something that they did not want to hear, or something that made them angry. Those clients who had done well on the therapy journey were the ones who returned to the next session and stated: *'I did not like what you said to me last session,',* or *'I was confused by your feedback about my ex-wife. I thought you would be on my side!'*

When my clients told me how they felt, we were able to discuss our different perspectives which strengthened our working relationship. If communication was an issue for my client in their life, we could use the interactions between us in the therapy room to increase my clients' confidence and awareness, which they could then use to improve their relationships outside the therapy room.

SUMMARY

In this chapter, we covered in depth what is required for effective communication that meets your needs. We looked at the different communication styles and their purposes, unpacked a communication formula and looked at how seeing a psychologist can raise your awareness of your communication style, as well as provide a great place to practise your assertiveness skills.

As a result of reading this chapter, I would encourage you to reflect on your own communication style and how it has served you thus far and give the communication formula a try in a safe setting.

Additional resources

Below are resources if you'd like further guidance or are in an unsafe situation:

Domestic Violence –1800 RESPECT: Confidential support and information to people experiencing violence and abuse. Support is available online and over the phone. www.1800respect.org.au; 1800 737 732.

Mensline: Free professional 24/7 counselling support for men concerned about mental health, anger management, family violence (using and experiencing), addiction, relationship, stress and wellbeing. Phone and online (including video) counselling available. www.mensline.org.au; 1300 78 99 78.

Headspace Australia: Assistance for young people aged 12-25, on topics such as: general mental health, physical health, work and study, alcohol and other drugs. Online and phone counselling, information and support. www.headspace.org.au.

Suicide Call Back Service: Free 24/7 counselling for suicide prevention and mental health via telephone, online and video for anyone affected by suicidal thoughts. www.suicidecallbackservice.org.au; 1300 659 467.

Kids Helpline: Free webchat and phone counselling for kids, teens, young adults, parents and carers and schools for any reason. www.kidshelpline.com.au; 1800 55 1800.

References

Alcohol and Drug Foundation. (2021) *'Having the Conversation'*. https://adf.org.au/talking-about-drugs/having-conversation/.

Harmsworth, C., & Paulmann, S. (2018). Emotional communication in long-term abstained alcoholics. *Alcoholism: Clinical and Experimental Research, 42*(9), 1715-1724. https://doi.org/10.1111/acer.13813

United States of America. Department of Health and Human Services; National Institutes of Health; National Institute on Drug Abuse (2022); *'How do drugs affect your brain?'*. https://teens.drugabuse.gov/drug-facts/brain-and-addiction#topic-2

Villines, Z. (2017, June 29). What does the frontal lobe do? *Medical News Today.* http://www.medicalnewstoday.com/articles/318139.

Chapter 10

The Power of Intentionality

'All that counts in life is intention.'

– Andrea Bocelli

In Chapter 8, we discussed that progress in therapy can be difficult to notice. At the same time, it is important to approach your treatment with intentionality.

Good news

There are some objective ways for psychologists to track progress in therapy in order to ensure that you are heading in the right direction and getting closer to your goals. The section below will introduce a number of common questionnaires and tools that psychologists frequently use during the course of treatment for this purpose.

Why is this important?

'If you can measure it, you can manage it.'
— **Unknown**

As you have hopefully gathered by now, psychology is a science. A big part of psychologists' training and work is research. In fact, there are psychologists and other mental health professionals who not only provide talking therapy to clients, but they also conduct research in their area of interest. This can also involve designing and testing different scales and questionnaires that measure symptoms of various psychological conditions. For example, the Beck Depression Inventory (1961) and the Beck Anxiety Inventory (1990), were both developed by the psychiatrist Dr. Aaron Beck and his colleagues. You may recall that Aaron Beck is also the founder of CBT. He worked with depressed patients, conducted research on the topic of depression and the effectiveness of CBT and created inventories that were relevant to his work with his patients (Beck Institute, 2022).

There are many questionnaires, tests and inventories that have been developed in the field of psychology – ranging from IQ tests to personality tests to ability tests and more. Psychological tests and scales are used for different purposes, such as assessment, diagnosis or assisting people to decide what job would suit them. The broad topic of psychological testing is beyond the scope of this book. I have included information at the end of the chapter for those who are interested to explore this further.

The Power of Intentionality

This chapter will focus on the uses of questionnaires and inventories in the context of therapy where the aim is specifically to track the client's progress.

Some benefits of the questionnaires used in therapy

- Tracking seemingly negligible progress using objective metrics makes it easier for the client to keep up motivation in the short and longer term.
- The questionnaires have been researched and tested to ensure that they are valid and reliable.
- Results of the questionnaires give the therapist an indication whether the strategies that they are using are making a difference.
- Lack of progress could indicate that it may be appropriate to change strategies or to involve additional specialists (e.g., psychiatrists) during treatment.

In my work, I have found that the use of assessment questionnaires was a great indicator whether therapy alone was making a difference in reducing the client's unwanted symptoms. A long time ago, I had a client in their mid-20's who really hoped that talking therapy alone would help reduce their symptoms of depression. The client and I agreed to try talking therapy for a number of sessions, monitoring their progress using one of the assessment tools. I administered the tool on their first session and again at their sixth session.

When I compared the results of both questionnaires, they were exactly the same. Even though my client attended every session, completed all their assigned homework and was highly motivated to achieve their desired goal, in their specific case, therapy alone did not result in a reduction of their unwanted symptoms. Considering these results, my client and I had to discuss additional options, such as trying a course of antidepressant medication. I wrote an updating letter to their GP and included their scores from the first and the second assessment, as well as a recommendation to discuss the option of medication as an adjunct to therapy. Without the use of the questionnaire, this client possibly would have wasted many weeks or months putting in a lot of effort and having high hopes that therapy alone would work for them, when, in their case, additional interventions were needed.

Common assessment scales and questionnaires

Below you will find the most common assessment questionnaires that I use in my work. Other psychologists may use different questionnaires or assessment tools, depending on who they are working with and what they need to assess. In my case, I work mainly with patients who present with symptoms of stress, depression and anxiety. Many of my clients are referred by their GPs, so I use the most common assessment tools that focus on stress, depression and anxiety and that GPs are familiar with:

- **The K10:** The Kessler Psychological Distress Scale is a simple self-report questionnaire which measures general psychological distress and includes 10 questions relating to symptoms of depression and anxiety with a five-level response scale. The K10 is a common tool that GPs in Australia administer to their patients when they create a Mental Health Care Plan for them to see a psychologist. This gives the GP and the psychologist the patient's base score of their level of distress at the time of the referral, before beginning any psychological treatment. In my practice, I get the patient to complete the K10 in our sixth session and again in our tenth session. I provide the GP with progress reports, where I include the

patient's K10 score from each session and compare it to the base score at the time of referral. Once again, this gives an indication of the progress made by the patient.
- **The DASS-21:** Depression, Anxiety and Stress Scale – 21 items (DASS-21) is a set of three self-reporting scales designed to measure the emotional states of depression, anxiety and stress (Lovibond & Lovibond, 1995). In my opinion, the DASS-21 is a very comprehensive measurement tool and is one of my favourites as it provides a quick snapshot of my clients' levels of each emotional state.
- **Beck Depression Inventory (BDI) and Beck Anxiety Inventory (BAI):** As mentioned earlier, both of these inventories were developed by Aaron Beck. They are great measurement tools, but the BDI is a relatively long questionnaire to complete – about three pages. I have found that many clients who have symptoms of severe depression struggle to complete it. However, it is very detailed, so if I need a comprehensive indicator of my client's level of depression, I use the BDI.

Important facts about these measurement tools

The tools are as follows:

- Self-reported questionnaires, which are based entirely on the client's own perception of how they are going, not the therapist's perception. One might state that this could make them biased; however, the questionnaires are often used in combination with other clinical information, such as the clinical observations of the practitioner and the information that the client reports in the sessions. In my work, I have had occasions when I could see that the client was unable to accurately complete the questionnaire, either due to the severity of their psychological symptoms, memory difficulties or comprehension problems as a result of an intellectual disability. In those cases, I couldn't rely on the scores of the questionnaires, but observing the client completing the questionnaire gave me very valuable information about their psychological state and challenges, which I could use as part of my assessment. For other clients who are well enough to complete the questionnaires, the scores provide important information from session to session and over time as to how the person is feeling and if there is a reduction in their symptoms.

- They are just a snapshot of what is happening right now. A client might have had a rough week or just a really bad day which would be reflected in their scores. It can be disheartening to see that drop in their scores if they feel that they are improving overall. In two weeks or two months, their results could look completely different. What is important is the general trend of the results **over a longer period of time**. For example, do the results generally: stay the same, increase or decrease over a few months? It is a little bit like watching the stock market. Minute-by-minute and hour-by-hour, there could be many changes happening. However, what is significant is the general trend of the market over the longer term.

I'll share with you a couple of stories to demonstrate the benefits of these measurements.

In one example, I was working with a client during a period when they felt really low. I got them to complete the DASS-21. Their results indicated severe levels on all three scales: depression, anxiety and stress. This was our base score. Two months later, I re-administered the DASS-21. My client could not believe it. Their scores across all three scales were in the normal range! The way that it happened is that two months prior, my client outlined the goals that he wanted to achieve. We did not put a timeframe on the goals but started actively working on them. I gave my client homework, which he completed between sessions, then reported back to me. Neither the client nor I expected to see such a dramatic difference in the scores, but those scores affirmed the extent of the progress that they made in two months and motivated them to stay on track.

Another client of mine struggled with anxiety for a long time. It took a combination of deep inner work in therapy, support from their medical team and a combination of medications for this client's anxiety symptoms to decrease from a severe level to a normal level. The client did not notice a change in their anxiety themselves, but the scores clearly showed a steady decrease in the severity of symptoms over time. It is only thanks to us using the assessment questionnaires that my client had tangible evidence that what they were doing was working.

These examples demonstrate the value of having something external to the therapist and the client to monitor levels of distress, as how we feel internally is not always an accurate indicator.

What if?

- **Your therapist is not using any measurement tools**

    Not all therapists do, and they are not always necessary. I don't use measurement tools with every client. I will now take this opportunity to dispel another myth about seeing a psychologist: there does *not* need to be a specific problem or a concerning behaviour to bring you to a psychologist. I have clients who attend sessions because they are looking for a 'sounding board'. They are mentally healthy people who simply want to debrief on usual events in their lives with an objective person and receive a different perspective on their lives. In their case, they do not have anything tangible for us to 'work on' and as such there is also no 'progress' to track. So, not all cases require the use of assessment questionnaires.

Additionally, there may be things that you would like to work on but there may not be specific assessment tools available for those particular issues. For example, you may wish to increase your confidence in standing up to bullies at work or at school. To my knowledge, there aren't any formal assessments available for an issue this specific, but if this is what you wish to work on, you and your therapist can discuss and agree on how to measure your progress in this area. One of my clients had this exact goal: to stand up to a bully. In the session, we went over all the emotional, physical, behavioural and social indicators that would tell my client that they were heading in the right direction. This gave my client specific indicators that they could keep track of and report back to me so we could celebrate their progress.

- **Your mood and symptoms change often**

  As mentioned earlier, questionnaires only take a 'snapshot'. It is like taking a quick photo of how you are this very minute. If you take a photo of yourself once per month, the clothes that you are wearing, your hairstyle and your mood is likely to be different in each photograph. However, if you then decide to look at your photos from the first photo that you took to the photo 12 months later, you may see differences between them that you wouldn't have noticed otherwise. This is the same with the progress questionnaires. Their purpose is to track changes *over time* and also make adjustments in real time if that's required.

Additional ways to track your progress

- Noticing reactions of the people you trust. I always ask my clients whether people around them, like close friends and family, noticed any difference in them. People might make comments about positive changes in your behaviour, which is a great indication that therapy is working. If people close to you bring up negative changes in your behaviour while you're seeing a therapist, I would raise this with your therapist. Not everyone will support you becoming more confident and stronger emotionally, so to ensure that your environment does not impact on your progress, bring up any negative reactions you are receiving in the session.

- Noticing whether things that were scary or anxiety-provoking in the past are easier now. Often, these are really small things, like being more confident to make a phone call, deciding not to do something out of an obligation or confronting someone who you were hesitant to confront in the past. In the case of my client whose goal was to stand up to a bully, they recognised that they were making progress as they observed that: they were more assertive when they were communicating with the person, their voice was steady, their mind was clear and they felt empowered after the experience. Thus, even without a formal measurement scale, the client had specific and tangible indicators to go by to track how they were going with their goal.

SUMMARY:

In this chapter, we looked at objective ways to track your progress in therapy through the use of assessment questionnaires. I introduced the most common questionnaires that I use in my work and gave examples to demonstrate the benefits of using such questionnaires, both for the client and the therapist. I also outlined other ways to track your progress, such as by deciding on objective 'success parameters' with your therapist and noticing positive feedback from supportive loved ones.

In the next chapter, we will shift gear and look at the process of change and how to assist a loved one who may not wish to get assistance.

Additional information:

For general information on psychological testing, visit the American Psychological Association's website: www.apa.org/topics/testing-assessment-measurement/understanding.

References:

Beck Institute. (2022). https://www.beckinstitute.org

Lovibond, S.H, & Lovibond, P.F. (1995). Manual for the Depression Anxiety & Stress Scales. (2nd Ed.) Sydney: Psychology Foundation.

Chapter 11

The Power of Stepping Back

Most of the chapters in this book focus on the reader recognising something about themselves that needs to change and then taking the initiative to effect that change. However, there are times in our lives when our primary concern is not ourselves, but someone else who is close to us and who we care about: a friend, child, parent or someone else.

'Helping others isn't a chore; it is one of the greatest gifts there is.'
– Liya Kebede

This chapter will focus on those loved ones who **don't see that they need help or refuse to accept professional help**. These situations can be incredibly stressful for concerned family members and friends.

The natural desire to help our loved ones

During my psychology studies, I worked for six years as a Helpline Advisor with the national mental health charity SANE Australia. By far the most common enquiry that the callers had was: *'I am concerned about my friend /family member. I believe that they need psychological assistance but they do not wish to get help. What can I do and how can I get them to get help?'*

Seeing a loved one struggling and unsure of where to turn would naturally bring up feelings of distress and helplessness. It can be especially challenging when the person's behaviour is confusing and interfering with other people's day-to-day activities. The loved ones might be wondering why the person cannot see the damage that their behaviour is causing for themselves and for others and more importantly: why would they not want to change?

The desire to push the person to get help would be strong at this point and the loved ones might even consider the option for psychological or psychiatric help to be forced upon the person without their consent. Those feelings of frustration and helplessness are understandable.

Helping those who may not want to help themselves

First, let's go over the basics. By now, you will have read 10 chapters of this book on how to get help for yourself. What have you learned?

The Power of Stepping Back

To change one's behaviour, a few things need to be present:

- **Awareness** of the behaviour that needs to be changed
- **Inner desire** to change the behaviour
- **Motivation** to do something different, to step out of the comfort zone
- **Determination** to stick to a new way of doing something

Change is difficult and uncomfortable. Not many people want to admit that they need to change. Change is also scary and requires a lot of effort. Reflect on the behaviours that you wanted to change. What did it take to motivate you to take the first step?

For many people, **it takes a crisis to change their behaviour, or a strong ultimatum from a loved one.** Even when such conditions are present, the person might still not be fully ready to take the required steps to change a certain behaviour.

On the next page, you will see a diagram that outlines the stages a person goes through on their journey towards change. It is based on the work by reserachers James Prochaska and Carlo DiClemente (1983).

What's Normal Anyway

The Cycle of Change (Prochaska & DiClemente; 1983)

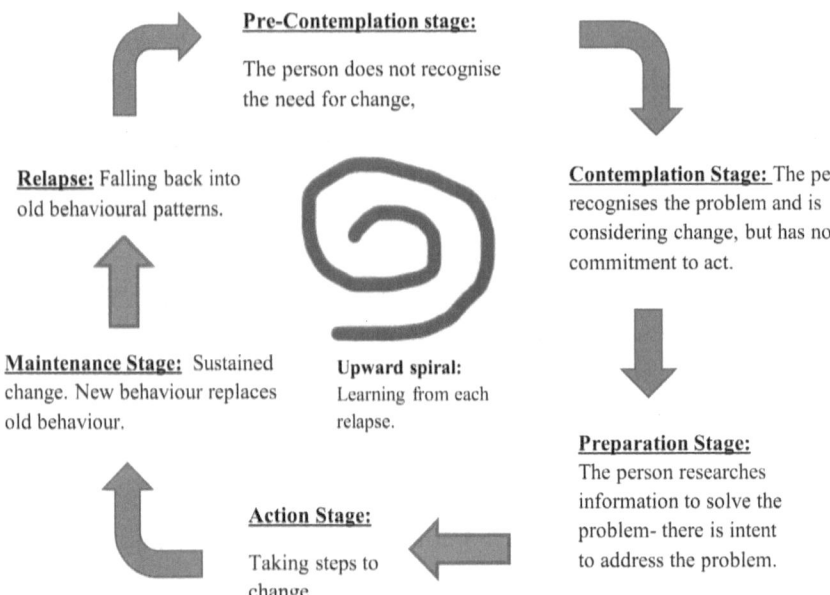

As you can see from the diagram, there are a number of stages that the person needs to go through in order to even decide to make a change. Sometimes external pressures are required. For example, when people are mandated to attend counselling because a judge ordered for them to do so. However, the most powerful change, the one that lasts the longest is the change that the person decides to make for themselves. When they decide that it is time.

Now, let's go back to the loved one whom you are concerned about.

Forcing someone to change

It is something that is very difficult to do and if it happens by using such methods as threats, ultimatums and manipulation, it is unlikely to be sustainable and can be counterproductive.

The Power of Stepping Back

This is a bitter pill to swallow when you have good intentions. Ultimately, however, your loved one has the right to decide how they are going to live. At the end of the day, the only person you can change is yourself.

We will discuss in this chapter ways that you could communicate with your loved one to increase the chances that they will understand your concerns for them and will possibly agree to take some steps. However, there is no guarantee of this, as your loved one has their own desires, thoughts and goals for themselves that may not match what you think is best for them.

Exceptions to the rule and when forcible treatment can be given

You may remember from Chapter 5 that the health industry is the most regulated industry in the world and there are many laws that govern it. Getting someone to receive medical treatment against their will would occur only in very specific situations.

Different countries have their own laws, of course. In Australia, we have legislation called the *Mental Health Act (2014)*. In essence, this legislation stipulates that for someone to be forced treatment against their will certain criteria needs to apply, such as **the person's behaviour being an imminent threat to themselves or to someone else**. These laws are very strict, as by forcing someone to get medical treatment against their will, we are breaching their personal liberties. SANE Australia's factsheet *Involuntary Treatment* (www.sane.org/information-stories/facts-and-guides/involuntary-treatment) describes this in more detail. If your loved one does fall into the category of being an imminent threat to themselves or to someone else, it may be a good idea to familiarise yourself with crisis services in your local area. Where I live and work, the standard practice is to get in contact with the local Crisis Assessment and Treatment Team (CATT) based within local hospitals. It is a good idea to look up details of your local hospital and the details of the local CATT *before* a crisis occurs. This way you can familiarise yourself with their services and get information about when it's appropriate for you to contact them.

If your loved one does not fall under the criteria of involuntary treatment, there are still things that you can do to keep the communication lines open and perhaps gently encourage them to reach out for assistance.

Steps to take to help others

Step 1: Depending on the person and your relationship with them, if it is safe to do so, the first step would be to communicate your concerns to the person in a calm, objective manner. Please use your judgement and if physical or emotional safety is a concern, skip this step and contact the support services listed at the end of this chapter.

If you do wish to try calm communication, Chapter 9 comprehensively outlined tips for doing so, which can be summarised as follows:

- Discussions work best when the people involved have had enough food, water and rest, if possible.
- Ensure that the person is in a state of mind where they are able to take in your feedback.
- Keep your feedback to objective observations of behaviour with a clear indication of what you are asking from them.

The Power of Stepping Back

Examples:

'I felt concerned yesterday when I noticed you leaving the house after drinking alcohol, because you could have been involved in an accident. I would like for us to consult with a specialist.'

'I felt scared when you were yelling at me yesterday for making a mistake. I would like for us to see a relationship counsellor.'

Respond to the **emotion** that the person is expressing. For example, if someone is distressed and is using curse words, instead of focusing on the swearing, try to imagine what they might be feeling at this moment. You could say something like, *'I imagine that you're feeling upset right now,'* or, *'I guess if this had happened to me, I'd be pretty annoyed as well.'* Most of us want to feel understood and want to be seen. By empathising first with the person, the intensity of their emotion may gradually subside and they may be more willing to hear you out.

Step 2: Make an appointment with your GP to discuss your concerns.

Even if you and your loved one are seeing the same GP, if your loved one is an adult, due to privacy regulations, the doctor won't be able to talk to you about them. However, the doctor can hear out your concerns and may have suggestions for you.

Step 3: Get support and strategies from the organisations listed at the end of this chapter.

What's Normal Anyway

Potential concerns

1. What if my relative/friend becomes physically violent?

Violence is *never* acceptable, and you should not tolerate it from anyone. If in immediate danger, leave and phone 000, or the local emergency number in your country. Contact violence support services in your area and if in Australia, get in contact with 1800 RESPECT to devise a plan of action.

2. I am worried that my relationship with the person will deteriorate even more if I express my concerns to them.

If you are unsure how to approach the person, you may wish to consider speaking to a trusted doctor or qualified counsellor. The suggestions in the earlier parts of this book will assist you in deciding who you should talk to about your concerns.

3. My loved one is already seeing a mental health professional, but they are not telling them the truth!

I heard this statement often from concerned family members or friends. Yes, there is a strong likelihood that your loved one is not telling the whole story to the professional. According to Edward Teyber (2006), many people actually do not reveal important information to their psychologists. Apparently, it is normal!

The fact that your loved one is talking to a professional is already a step in the right direction. Please remember that each person has their own perception of events. In their sessions with the professional, your loved one will naturally focus on what is meaningful to *them*. Psychologists and other mental health professionals are not detectives, and they work with the information that is available, knowing that

The Power of Stepping Back

it can change from session to session and that new information can come to light from various sources. The professional may notice discrepancies in the person's story and probe for more details or seek further information from another health professional who is involved in their care, such as their GP.

You might feel frustrated and powerless looking at your loved ones from the sidelines and not being able to help to the extent that you would like to.

Focus on what you can do and what is realistically within your control

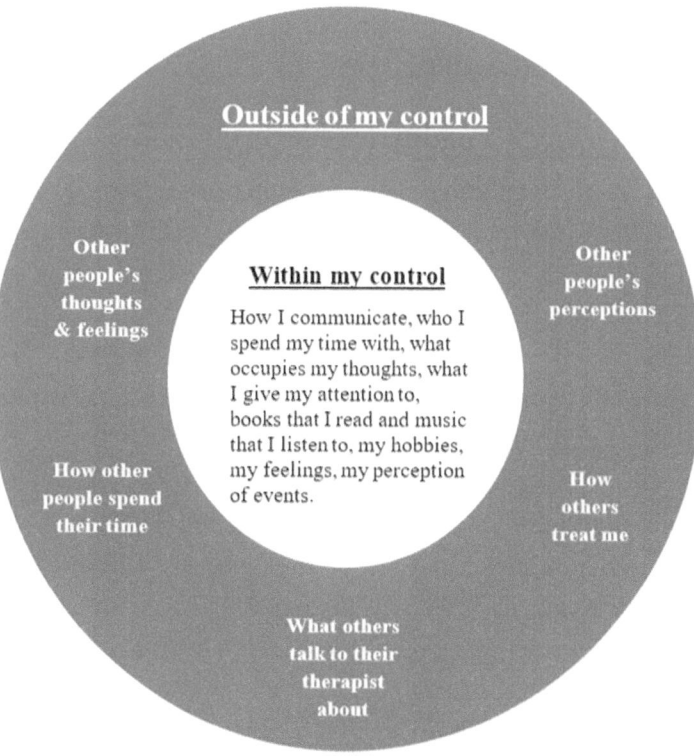

What's Normal Anyway

When in doubt, ask yourself: '*What **can** I do? What **is** in my control?*'

At times, the answer will be: '*You can go for a walk; you can talk to someone who understands; you can lie down for a nap; you can have a glass of water or make yourself a hot cup of tea; you can have a shower; you can listen to music that calms you down; you can pray; you can cry and release pent up emotions.* This might sound dismissive to a concerned relative or friend, as we often want to act and to 'fix' a situation. However, focusing on remaining calm, healthy, grounded and psychologically and emotionally sound is very important, both in terms of modelling healthy habits to our loved one and ensuring that we have the required energy and mental presence to fully be there for them as they navigate challenging situations.

Additional information/resources

Domestic Violence: 1800 RESPECT – Confidential support and information to people experiencing violence and abuse. Support is available online and over the phone. www.1800respect.org.au; 1800 737 732.

SANE Australia: Information and referral on mental illness, a free counselling service available via phone, web chat or e-mail. www.sane.org; 1800 18 7263.

Family Drug Help: Family Drug and Gambling Helpline providing practical help, information and support to families and friends affected by someone's drinking, drug use or gambling. Based in Victoria, Australia, the Helpline operates 24/7 on 1300 660 068. www.sharc.org.au.

References:

Teyber, E. (2006). *Interpersonal Process in Therapy: An Integrative Model* (5th ed.). Thompson Brooks/Cole.

Chapter 12

The Power of Self-Mastery

'Growth is the only evidence of life.'
— **John Henry Newman**

This book had taken you through the required steps to find the right professional for you to guide you on your self-development journey. In this chapter, we will look at what is, in my opinion, the ultimate goal of the self-development journey: becoming your own psychologist, therapist or mentor.

What's Normal Anyway

Why is this important?

As uncomfortable and scary it can be for clients, eventually, formal therapy will come to an end. Psychologists retire, move countries, and may change careers. That's why it is a good idea to have at least one of your self-development goals to become your own therapist. At the end of the day, you do really know yourself better than anyone else ever will. Your therapist's job is to give you a range of tools that may work effectively for you, and your job is to find what fits and make it a part of your daily routine as much as possible.

Did you know: **the bulk of therapy work is actually done between sessions, not during the session?** Therapy sessions tend to go for 50 to 60 minutes and often occur once a week or once a fortnight. What happens between the sessions is what makes the real difference in your life. It is not enough to get new information and learn new strategies. One must practise the strategies and implement them between the sessions to build confidence and see what works.

It is similar to signing up to go the gym or hiring a personal trainer. One hour of weightlifting or 30 minutes of an aerobics class will not make a big difference in the long run. However, if you work out multiple times a week and keep up that routine consistently, you are more likely to see results. The more you practise, the more confident you'll get and eventually you might not need the guidance of your personal trainer. A similar process happens in therapy, except that we work on strengthening the 'emotional muscle', and it grows stronger through regular practise.

The Power of Self-Mastery

Self-development and self-growth are a never-ending journey.

For as long as you live on planet Earth, there will always be something for you to discover and there will always be obstacles and new challenges. This is why you are here – to learn, to be challenged and to expand your understanding and perspective.

However, this does not at all mean that you'll be 'stuck' in therapy forever. From an ethical perspective, sessions with a therapist should continue only while they are clinically necessary and in the client's best interest. As this book is specifically focussed on people who *choose* to see a therapist, therapy can end whenever the person decides to. Often it happens when goals have been met or after discussion between the therapist and the client around how they feel that the client is progressing and when it is time for the treatment to come to an end.

Additionally, unless the therapist retires or changes careers, a client can absolutely continue seeing their therapist beyond the initially set goals and can also book sessions for 'maintenance' – maybe once every few months, or once a year. In fact, it is very common for my clients to schedule sessions with me once every three to six months to ensure that they are still on track. I liken these 'maintenance sessions' to half-yearly dental check-ups. This makes for a more gradual transition and gives clients a chance to build their confidence that they have the necessary tools and skills to cope with life events, while also knowing that they can make an appointment with their therapist if they struggle.

What's Normal Anyway

Becoming your own psychologist

This is my goal for every client: to become so confident in their own capacity to tackle their challenges and so proficient in utilising the tools that I have taught them that they become their own psychologist.

Sometimes, the journey towards becoming your own therapist will take six weeks, sometimes six months and sometimes six years. This all depends on the issue that brought you to therapy and the existing resources that you already have. From what I have noticed with my clients, reaching the point when they manage challenges without my input is a moment of real pride for them. To this day, I hear from clients whom I have not seen in many years, who send me a quick email to let me know that they are still tracking well. It is very heart-warming to receive these emails and is a testament to the hard work that they invested during therapy.

Leaving the therapy nest and venturing out on your own

Almost every client that I have, at some point in therapy expresses anxiety about losing the 'safety net' of our sessions. This is very normal and understandable.

This is what I say to every client in preparation for us finishing therapy:

'One day, months or years from now, you will forget absolutely everything that we discussed in our sessions. You will not remember any of the strategies or have only a faint memory of what we discussed. During times of crisis, you will revert back to the way you handled things before you started therapy. It will feel as though you are back at square one. This is because during times of stress, the brain naturally chooses the path that has been practised the most, the path of least resistance. Everyone is like that.

The Power of Self-Mastery

'However, you have spent many weeks with me practising new ways of doing things. So, you could never go back to square one ever again! Unless you have complete amnesia, all the information is there. You might need one or two refresher sessions and you'll be right on track'.

An important point to remember is that the information that your psychologist imparted on you is not new. All of the current strategies used in modern psychology are out there in many different forms, often available in self-help books, workshops and on reputable websites. In fact, the more you expose yourself to the same information presented in different ways, the better, as the same topic can be tackled from different angles, and you are bound to learn something new.

For example, I love the topic of anxiety and have attended countless workshops on it over the last 20 years. Even though I believe that I have a lot of knowledge on this topic, I still keep attending workshops on anxiety. Why? Because every presenter has his or her own style and explores the topic from a different angle. Some presenters focus on the neurobiological aspects of anxiety, some focus on facts and interesting new research, other presenters teach breathing exercises and relaxation techniques. It is all valuable and I pick up new tips and strategies from every presentation.

Steps towards self-mastery

1. **Practise the strategies** that your psychologist recommends. Most of the behaviours that you need assistance with have been learned and practised for many years, or even decades. It takes practise to master something new.

2. **Embrace mistakes** and remember that you cannot fail at self-development.

Even under the guidance of a psychologist, at times, clients add their own flavour to techniques and see for themselves whether or not their adjustments have worked. Embrace the fact that you will be learning for the rest of your life and that mistakes give you a chance to improve and try again.

3. **Continue to grow and develop** by attending workshops, seminars, taking online courses and watching documentaries that relate to the areas of self-development. There are many interest groups online and a lot of support groups that you can in attend in person. Creating a network of likeminded people who share the same goal of self-improvement can be invaluable. Being a part of a network has benefits such as learning new information, celebrating each other's progress and uplifting one another if things get challenging.

4. **Celebrate your progress.** This is a very important step and one that I noticed many people skip. It is so important that I will expand on it below.

Celebrate your success

Very often people minimise or downplay their successes. Prior to doing something challenging people often feel fear and anxiety, but as soon as the event is over, most people move on with their lives without acknowledging what they overcame. I'll use an example of attending a job interview to demonstrate this. For most people, attending a job interview is anxiety-provoking. They decide what they'll wear, make sure that they attend the interview on time, wonder what questions will be asked and hope that they'll make a good impression. Once the interview is over, there is a big sigh of relief and often new worries start: *'I should have answered better; I'm not sure they liked me: I hope that I*

The Power of Self-Mastery

did well.' The person completely skips all the steps that got them to this point that took confidence, effort and courage such as: deciding to apply for a new role, creating or updating a resume, completing the application well enough to even get the interview and putting in all the effort in preparing for it. Whether or not the person gets the job, they have taken steps towards improving their financial situation. However, we as humans focus only on the outcome.

> *'Focus on the journey, not the destination. Joy is found not in finishing an activity but in doing it.'*
> **– Greg Anderson**

When it comes to attending therapy, notice how many chapters I have devoted in this book to normalising people's doubts and anxieties about taking the first step towards seeking help. Then, there are multiple steps along the way to get out of your comfort zone, share vulnerabilities with a stranger and trial unfamiliar ways of thinking and behaving. **Yet, as soon as people get through each challenging step, they consciously or unconsciously act as if it was nothing and are eager to get to the next stage.** This is how we miss out on life. We constantly rush towards *'what's next?'* without giving ourselves credit for how far we have come.

Your goal could be to reach the top of the mountain, and if the mountain is very high, it's especially important to ensure that from time to time you pause, have a drink of water and admire the view for a few minutes. Maybe take a selfie with the view in the background. I would encourage you to get into the habit of taking 'progress snapshots' of yourself frequently and normalise congratulating yourself even if you think that your achievements are 'nothing special'. Get into the habit of noticing what you're doing right. All of this self-acknowledgement adds up.

What's Normal Anyway

I love this quote by Louise Hay: *'You have been criticising yourself for years and it hasn't worked. Try approving of yourself and see what happens.'*

In this spirit, let's briefly practise. Right now, this very minute, stop and reflect on the past week. See whether there was anything that you had done that was outside of your comfort zone. It can be the tiniest thing, and something that another person who knows your deepest fears and struggles and who wants to celebrate your wins with you would have noticed. If any of the exercises in this book challenged you, yet you still completed them, you can count them as well:

_____
_____
_____
_____
_____
_____
_____
_____
_____

Anchor the experience

With some achievements, you may even wish to take a step further to make them more memorable, like treating yourself to a massage, a meal at your favourite restaurant, or giving yourself a gift to remind you of this moment. When I finished my first draft of this book, I almost fell into the same trap of *'just keep going'* as the book wasn't published yet! I forgot how much time, effort and courage it had taken me to even embark on this new adventure. I needed to remind myself to stop, and I decided that I must mark this milestone somehow. I thought for a bit what would be a memorable way to acknowledge

The Power of Self-Mastery

finishing the first draft and since my achievement was related to writing I decided that I'd treat myself by getting some new stationery! I went to a stationery store that I love to browse and allowed myself to savour the whole experience of being there. Without rushing myself, I walked around looking at notepads, journals and colourful pens and took in the sights and smells. I tested out different pens and highlighters, going for colours I would not normally try. This was, after all, a special occasion, so 'plain' pens and highlighters wouldn't do. In the end, I bought myself a few cool, unusual highlighters, a pretty pen and a new diary. Now, every time I look at this specific stationery, I smile because it reminds me of the occasion that prompted me to get them. Have fun, get creative. Match your rewards to your milestones as much as possible. Really savour celebrating yourself and your achievements.

SUMMARY

Life is a never-ending journey. Eventually, your formal therapy will come to an end, but your life learning will continue. Embrace the journey of self-development, remember to pause from time to time, enjoy the view and celebrate your efforts and achievements. This book is only the beginning.

Afterword

Congratulations! You have reached the end of the book. I hope that in doing so, you have expanded your current level of awareness and understanding of psychological issues. I also hope that you are now better equipped to recognise that the concept of 'normal' is relative, and what is considered normal for a person depends upon various factors.

You may remember the quick self-assessment that you completed in the beginning of this book. Now it is time for you to rate your level of awareness and knowledge once again, then compare your total scores. Based on these ratings, you may wish to re-read the relevant chapters or use the additional resources to get more information.

What's Normal Anyway

Level of awareness/knowledge after completing this book

Topic	Level of awareness/knowledge from 0-10
What is considered 'normal'?	
Signs that indicate that an assistance from a mental health professional is required	
Where to start in order to get professional help	
What other help is out there in addition to seeing a professional one-on-one	
Difference between psychologists, psychiatrists, counsellors, psychotherapists and life coaches	
Different types of psychological therapies that are currently available	
How to recognise that the mental health professional you are seeing is right for you	
Effective communication at home, at work or with friends and loved ones	
How to track your progress in therapy	
How and where to get help for a loved one	
How to become your own psychologist	
Helpful books, websites and articles that can further expand your knowledge	
Add up your scores for your total:	

About the Author

Yelena Fishman was born and raised in Kishinev, Moldova, until the age of nine when she emigrated to Israel with her parents and sister, where she developed social anxiety and depression due to years of bullying. A book that she read at age 15 helped her to overcome these challenges and ignited her passion for psychology. At the age of 19, Yelena emigrated to Melbourne, Australia to be reunited with her maternal grandparents and extended family.

In Australia, Yelena was able to fulfill her dream of becoming a psychologist. Yelena holds a Bachelor of Arts and a Postgraduate Diploma of Psychology from Monash University, and a Master of Counselling Psychology from Swinburne University. Yelena is a fully registered psychologist with the Australian Health Practitioners Regulations Agency (AHPRA) and is a member of the Australian Association of Psychologists Inc (AAPi).

What's Normal Anyway

Throughout her 15 years of counselling practice, Yelena has assisted hundreds of clients in overcoming their darkest and most challenging moments.

She has worked as a psychologist at non-for-profit organisations, primary schools, corporations and in medical centres in Melbourne. At present, she continues to assist her existing clients on a part-time basis and is excited about opportunities to share information on psychology to a broader audience. In the near future, Yelena plans to translate *'What's Normal Anyway?'* into Russian to further broaden its reach.

Yelena's Contact Details

Email: whats_normal_anyway@outlook.com
Website: www.yelena-fishman.com.au

Acknowledgements

Many friends and colleagues have helped me by reviewing this book and helping me improve it. In particular, I wish to thank my long-time colleague, Peter Langdon, a counselling and clinical psychologist, for his input and expertise. I also wish to thank Vania Tantirimudalige Don, Heather Binns and Sue Usher, who proofread this book.

I wish to thank my editor, Isabelle Russell, for her assistance.

A special thanks goes to my parents, partner and extended family for their unwavering support throughout this process.

Yelena Fishman

BA, PGDipPsych, MPsych(Couns)

Yelena Fishman is a psychologist, parent, and published author. She is highly sought after for her professional insights and unique approach to reduce unhelpful thoughts and uncomfortable feelings; and help her clients regain hope that life can be better.

An engaging and down to earth speaker, Yelena shares her 15 years of counselling experience, as well as personal experience of overcoming bullying, depression and social anxiety during her teenage years.

Yelena believes that personal struggles are a steppingstone towards something great. She is available to speak on the following topics.

The Power of Your Story

- Uncover the magic in your circumstances
- Turn any setback into triumph
- Create a life that you're proud to live

The Shocking Truth About Anxiety

- 3 lies that your anxiety likes to tell you
- Why anxiety is the best thing that ever happened to you
- Becoming the boss of your anxiety

How to Feel Cool, Calm and Collected in 5 Minutes

- Your brain in action
- Simple, effective steps we all know but miss!
- Surprising shortcuts to stop your racing thoughts in their tracks.

Contact Yelena at

whats_normal_anyway@outlook.com

to enquire about her speaking at your event, availability and rates.

Notes

What's Normal Anyway

Notes

What's Normal Anyway

Notes

www.ingramcontent.com/pod-product-compliance
Lightning Source LLC
Chambersburg PA
CBHW021435080526
44588CB00009B/536